Why Are You So Long and Sweet?

Collected Long Poems of

David W. McFadden

SOME OTHER BOOKS BY THE AUTHOR

The Poem Poem (Weed/Flower, 1967)
Letters from the Earth to the Earth (Coach House, 1969)
The Great Canadian Sonnet (Coach House, 1970, 1971)
Poems Worth Knowing (Coach House, 1971)
The Ova Yogas (Weed/Flower, 1972)
Intense Pleasure (McClelland & Stewart, 1972)
A Knight in Dried Plums (McClelland & Stewart, 1975)
The Poet's Progress (Coach House, 1977)
The Saladmaker (Cross Country, 1977)
On the Road Again (McClelland & Stewart, 1978)
I Don't Know (Vehicule, 1978)
A New Romance (Cross Country, 1979)
A Trip Around Lake Erie (Coach House, 1980)
A Trip Around Lake Huron (Coach House, 1980)
My Body Was Eaten by Dogs: Selected Poems of David McFadden
(McClelland & Stewart, 1982)
Country of the Open Heart (Longspoon, 1982)
Three Stories & Ten Poems (Prototype, 1982)
Animal Spirits (Coach House, 1983)
A Pair of Baby Lambs (The Front, 1983)
The Art of Darkness (McClelland & Stewart, 1984)
Canadian Sunset (Black Moss, 1986)
Gypsy Guitar (Talonbooks, 1987)
A Trip Around Lake Ontario (Coach House, 1988)
Anonymity Suite (McClelland & Stewart, 1992)
There'll Be Another (Talonbooks, 1995)
An Innocent in Ireland (McClelland & Stewart, 1995)
An Innocent in Scotland (McClelland & Stewart, 1999)
Five Star Planet (Talonbooks, 2002)
An Innocent in Newfoundland (McClelland & Stewart, 2003)
An Innocent in Cuba (McClelland & Stewart, 2005)
Why Are You So Sad? Selected Poems of David W. McFadden (Insomniac, 2007)
Be Calm, Honey (Mansfield, 2008)

Why Are You So Long and Sweet?
Collected Long Poems of
David W. McFadden

edited by Stuart Ross

INSOMNIAC PRESS

Editor for the press: Paul Vermeersch
Edited by Stuart Ross
Cover photo by William McFadden
Introduction copyright © Stuart Ross 2010
Poems copyright © David W. McFadden 2010
All poems in this book are reproduced by permission of the author

Library and Archives Canada Cataloguing in Publication

McFadden, David, 1940-
    Why are you so long and sweet? : collected long poems / of
David W. McFadden.

ISBN 978-1-897178-93-5

    I. Title.

PS8525.F32A6 2010   C811'.54   C2010-900664-X

The publisher gratefully acknowledges the support of the Canada Council,
the Ontario Arts Council, and the Department of Canadian Heritage
through the Book Publishing Industry Development Program.

Printed and bound in Canada

Insomniac Press
520 Princess Ave.
London, Ontario, Canada, N6B 2B8
www.insomniacpress.com

  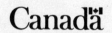

This book is for
Merlin Homer

Contents

Introduction

by Stuart Ross

> *Before a long poem*
> *a poet can only stand in stupid ignorance,*
> *knowing only kindness must be shown to words,*
> *his mindlessness steeped in a simple divinity.*
> *Poetry is a man sitting alone in a room*
> *with a ticking clock, the poet the mere tip*
> *of an ancient pyramid.*

— David W. McFadden, "I Don't Know"

David McFadden's magic comes perhaps from his humbleness before language, before poetry. Every line he writes is a celebration of the very fact that poetry exists, that we all exist, that we have language. He is indeed kind to words; he seems almost grateful to them. And especially in the long poems, McFadden approaches the page with a clear mind, a mindlessness, and lets his breathing and the words carry him, likely to a place that surprises him as much as it surprises us.

This book is the companion volume to *Why Are You So Sad? Selected Poems of David W. McFadden*, published in 2007 by Insomniac Press. It brings together the spiritual, surreal, often beautifully meandering epics that Dave wrote primarily from the mid-1960s through the early 1980s. *Why Are You So Long and Sweet? Collected Long Poems of David W. McFadden* also offers up some exciting bonus material: the newly discovered long poem "Nevada Standstill," which Dave unearthed shortly before this book's deadline, and a not-so-long but entirely engaging and never-before-collected poem from 1961, "Danny

Quebec," written when the poet was about twenty.

McFadden is enjoying something of a renaissance these days, as he approaches his seventieth birthday. *Why Are You So Sad?* was one of three books shortlisted for the 2008 Canadian Griffin Poetry Prize (when Robin Blaser was announced the winner at the gala, Dave turned to me and said, grinning, "You could have edited it better"). And his playful and poignant 2008 sonnet collection, *Be Calm, Honey*, from Mansfield Press, was shortlisted for the 2009 Governor General's Literary Award for Poetry. So these are busy times for a poet in his sixth decade of writing and publishing.

While a lot of poets would have been content letting an editor do all the work constructing a Selected or Collected, Dave got his claws into this one, just as he had with *Why Are You So Sad?* In some of the poems here he made only slight "corrections"; for others, he recreated entire passages. Whether he was just making corrections, or making the poems fresh for himself again, or simply being mischievous on occasion, for a lifelong McFadden fan like me, this was exhilarating.

Perhaps the most altered poem here is the magnificent "Night of Endless Radiance," where, amid the myriad changes, "the Stanley Cup" becomes "the Stan Bevington Cup." In "A New Romance," "the night as firm as a loving muscle" becomes "the night as firm as a farm in France." Other poems, like "Country of the Open Heart," received only moderate revision: mostly a tightening, an application of precision. And "The Cow That Swam Lake Ontario" has some new stanza breaks. For those fortunate enough to have the original editions, there's a lot of fun in comparing the texts, watching David McFadden of 2010 collaborate with David McFadden of 1967 or 1982.

Another thrill for the reader here is the previously unpublished "Nevada Standstill." It brings to Dave's oeuvre a tone I haven't seen anywhere else. No idea why this poem, with its intriguing title (the meaning of which the author himself doesn't quite recall) never found its way into a book before, but I'm sure glad McFadden dug it up and dusted it off while we were working on this volume. And then there's "Danny Quebec," which first appeared in 1961 in the still-thriving *PRISM international*. Dave remembered this one *after* our deadline, and the current editors of *PRISM* were kind enough to dig it out of the vaults and send us a PDF. Dave, who hadn't seen the poem for decades, wrote to me, "It's much better than I thought it would be, considering I was a mere child at the time and very foolish but definitely not as stupid as I thought I was after fifty years." "Danny Quebec" isn't a long poem at all, but it is longish, and for the McFadden enthusiast, it's a treasure.

Two of the poems here — "The Poem Poem" and "The Ova Yogas" — originally appeared as beautifully mimeographed chapbooks from poet/publisher/bookseller Nelson Ball's legendary Weed/Flower press. For some insight into the era and the scene, I urge readers to get hold of the late artist Barbara Caruso's two volumes of journals, *A Painter's Journey: 1966–1973* and *A Painter's Journey, Volume II: 1974–1979*, both from The Mercury Press. Barbara, who was the lifelong partner of Nelson Ball, has left an extraordinarily valuable document of a rich era in Canadian art and literature, with some nice cameo appearances by David McFadden.

Finally, an admission: this isn't strictly the *collected* long poems of David W. McFadden. Four more appear in *Why Are You So Sad?* — "Holy Days in a Lake Huron Resort Village," "Four Experiments," "Nature" and "Jane and Jean." Gather those up, snug 'em tight against this volume, and there you have it: the Complete Collected. Blame the overlap on my impatience of a few years ago. I couldn't wait for a book (this one) that I wasn't certain would ever appear.

While Dave hasn't written a long poem since "Cow Swims Lake Ontario," the 2002 rewrite of "The Cow That Swam Lake Ontario," he's been writing his poems in series for a couple of decades now. So while the poems in books such as *Gypsy Guitar*, *Five Star Planet* and *Be Calm, Honey* can be read individually, the entire works can also be read as long poems. Either way, like the eleven poems in this volume, for the reader approaching them mindlessly — or even mindfully — they offer intense pleasure.

The Poem Poem

"Fools have big wombs"
— William Carlos Williams

No one knows
                about my affair
                my pregnancy

the growing / so deep inside me

it is so flowerlike
a flower / inside me

                the cellular growth
of the poem, unseen
                point of beginning

flower / union of complex desires

A library? — how long
has this been here?
                a library
unfolding from a dream

a dream with petals

a flower and a library / touch
and illuminate a city

the incorporation of a poem /
put together like a city

No one knows
                the dream

that illuminates a city
by preceding it

It should pass soon
my nervousness

please forget
morning sickness

I will have everything
and nothing

I will hold it in my hand
like a rose

      it has come
a great distance
from conception

has the touch of the numerous
about it

     there are no numbers
     only light
         our growing

     volume after volume
     in our blackness

     No. 1
     all my power?

I need a place to write
let me try hard
to be buried
until I die

to stop my wondering
stop my stuttering
under the sky

get all the words
put them on the page
in hopeless perfection

I need love
regular income
flower pots.

It comes in my life
a perfect dream
that must be born

must find itself
outside me

walking away
from my corpse

The perfect length of a perfect poem

taking each syllable into account
and its complementary

each image,
its associative

poem of unravelling
bird-genealogy

"The Perfect Universe"

It's true it's flowerlike but it's more like a tree growing inside.
I thought of all the other mothers through time and felt small
then would look in a mirror and feel huge

The first three months you're weak like in sluggish winter
then the power comes as the baby increases in power
and you wonder at its security within the membranes

All through the nine months I could smell the earth
I was always conscious of things growing around me
and at times I could feel growth inside me

(In preparation my breasts
became great fruits)

this dream is a preparation

Nothing is separable

(it will always be inside me
as long as I'm alive)

This dream is too big!
I want to *scream!?!*

send showers of UFOs
out over the horizon

I'm on the road so much
I would be a perfect choice
for the saucers to contact

even the earth is getting fat
(with the dead)

(In Labour Expect the Worst
from the Italians
so free their screams /
so easy the birth

I felt so close
to other mothers)

... long before the
end of the universe
we will know all about it

there / it is ended
we are so laden with riches

doctor disallowed
my driving to F l o r i d a

coming onto the page
"the open hearth of language"

those glads there you see
were growing in Florida yesterday

glads with long stalks of buds in graduating phases of   openness

love is emptiness, emptiness, emptiness

(glads)

all the perfect poems ever written
two Hamilton Ontario men have been charged
with capital murder and attempted murder in Winnipeg
new cells penetrate into the limb buds causing them to elongate
some of the cells come to form a tri-segmented bone framework
five lobes appear

                    a toy forever
                                   put the ear
                   to the page
                                   and make
                    something of yourself

anecdotes about _____
(fill in name of your choice?)

that would certainly please Dante

("I am a five-year-old
  who swallowed a
  rhyming dictionary...")

Dante comes flying through the poetosphere
joyfully throws his arms around me

at the age of five months the fetus
has grown its full quota of nerve cells
all the individual will ever have
(12,000,000,000-plus)

"I am losing interest
in music" and women
poetry
        in the pop music field

        the human race is going places

        little epileptic fits in the womb
        the poor little thing outgrowing
        its food and oxygen supply
        enraged, suffocating, thrashing
        its way to freedom

        the word on the page

        All I have for you
        is a human flower

        Come under and under with me
        into the grave
        below the sewers
        below the deepest root
                find the

                word on the
                page

Under the spell of water

under the spell of radial static
(the wholly inhuman I)

(the water-world)

(alliterative underspell)

Note: German veterans won't be allowed to attend
the 1967 anniversary ceremonies at Dieppe /
a 92-year-old Alaskan does the sirshasana daily
doesn't have an aching bone in his body

radio waves from Alaska

after eight hours spent
listening to radio static
it's nice to get up
stretch your limbs

they were no soldiers but men
not men but gods
not gods but God
rare combinations of natural forces
radio static

slaughtered on ugly battlefields
dying cattle, groaning
for water

thanks for your thoughts

Global water circuitry

something magic there is
in the womb
that comprehends
language,

"The Electroencephalographic
Songbook"

Hold on there, oceans,

clouds, rivers and lakes,
streams, glaciers and cease.

Niagara Falls
Raingod's navel

STOP! for an
electromoment —
flow on !

lover of the
dry and deepest

because I am a !

Womanman !

inventor of the !
inhuman !

poem and wheel !

The watergod / god of the waters of the universe

Alderman McCullouch went to investigate
a homeowner's water pipe complaint —
found the complainant to be Alderman Kostyk
water pipes bursting all over
damage ran up to $2,000

Forebodings
            of our final resting place

                  to her death fourteen storeys below
                  in a Venetian canal
                  (sonnets)

The poets of the Vedas, the seers of the Upanishads
the sages who composed the Epics and the Puranas

the fish (and whales) of the Holy Bible

In 1613 CE Christ at last reached Niagara Falls

In another 2000 years of erosion the Falls
will have become mere rapids

Lake Erie will be a bog

(not taking into account
our technological spirit

man's supernatural powers
superhuman vision,

his path strewn with poems

I have an ambition someday

the loneliness inside my ears

to be a solar engineer but that
seems so far away
        keep this
        ring

        as a
        souvenir

        of our
        meeting

        meeting oh so
        briefly

        in a long life
        one who loves you

        so far away
        but life's too sad

        for me to worry
        what I be

        or who loves me
        or poetry

And no one's done it.
No one I know's done it.

Pound didn't, Shelley.
Blake or Shake-
Speare....

Attention all Gods!

I hope our children
have round faces

how I've loved
round faces

the ones I've loved
in my heart

the emotion
of love

largest army
ever seen
in Europe!

the poets etc.
of my short life.

hey all poets!
of eternity

in my womb
I find you
and your dreams

It has all happened at once
a trip to Niagara
April 1941

          the Faustian "spirit"
          (dream)
              each poet
          exposed his individuality
          by expressing his relation
          to Faust
              complaining
          about billboards separating
          wilderness without end
          from the highway, or

I am also an insatiable lover
said the doctor to Helen (of Troy)

(one afternoon on a long-sunk
isle of the Aegean)

(lover without end?)

Everything lives, cried he
in pure flame
          nothing can
die, he sighed

          No thing
          dies, watch

          old things turning
          inside out

This life inside me makes of me a box

that I may soon be emptied
realize my womanness again
in a variety of ways

We are dealing with the human!

the solar plexus as a TV receiver

things that grow inside me
to be born!
that my nun-existence
may be realized?

Human universe / my poor box
to grasp such

               as is asleep
               in this magnificent
               library

               deep in the woods
               enter
               by rolling away
               a big stone

               (see the book /
               part of a library)

Hey did you hear the one about the astrologer
who conducted
                    my stars is the boat setting out
so soon
            I would love

                        to write a universal history of food
                        that would be detail accurate
                        to my deepest vision of the subject
                        and serve a general readership
                        be studied by the world's fat
                        with pictures for the wide-eyed starving

                        is the bark so soon to sail
                        set out under the Greek moon
                        once and for all time

                        If I could feed
                        Bihar province,

                        come over from Kashmir
                        with a fifty-mile caravan of elephants

                        tied tail to trunk
                        heaped high with bags
                        of TV dinners (meatless)
                        Okanagan apples
                        Niagara peaches
                        Italian bread
                        Minute rice

                        screaming chickens

                        onions peppers wine

A continuous food-belt of elephants
between Benares and Rome —

as impossible in the universe
as it is in the poem

The New Jerusalem

       AWAKE!

       Traffic
       is moving in the streets!

       (kids
       are running home crying

what a funny place for a library!
I've been coming by here all my LIFE
and never noticed it before NOW

Oh if only I had noticed it before
how different would be my LIFE NOW

problem of understanding children

here in the New Jerusalem Library
we catalogue telepathically

like a child waking up to find he's alive
or those who seem to have been born awake

you mean you woke me just to tell me
Jack Ruby is dead?

trouble with writing poem poems
is they lead one into a superabundance
of magnetism. I see black clouds
forming, a natural lightning path
heading straight for my head

and I was not ready —
I was dreaming my old library dream
all The Invisibles were there

also The Inevitables. The cry went up:

FREE LITERATURE!

                    You smile! You understand!
                    Oh Joan how glorious

                    After the first few pages

                    of that play
                    I decided
                    I had
                    to become
                    an actor

                    bad apple
                    to bite

                    the apple's the thing
                    in period dress

In opening scene I'm in dress of brilliant feathers
and magic athletic support with powers-of-levitation
and I go flying out from behind fallen curtains
out flapping with solemn glee over heads of audience

and my heartbeat is electrically amplified throughout theatre
program notes advising audience to synchronize their beats with mine

and with Biblical ecstasy my bejewelled voice emerges
foretelling the coming of murderous alien races
bespeaking need to bury our knowledge
suppress our powers so imperfectly perfected, or

don't talk to me of the Death Wish
I'm only interested in death

I wish only for a perfect baby,
it means the end of me
from my point of view, or

I know not what I am
or in which world I dwell
I only know my solar
plexus, see it swell

                              going on for
how many years it's impossible to tell

The Devonian and early Carboniferous beaches
were strewn with holocausts of freaks

a detailed history
of the billion years before man

the fiery sermons of Rev. Featherstone
He has returned from Viet Nam a changed man!

Ho hum!

there are enough people concerned with Man
all that unnatural flowering
I was taught early to hate

and untaught / taught / untaught

like me, in the sun, bright beaches

that are now in the middle of the Gobi.
Beautiful Britain books

man never did fall
but he should have.

Again that explo-
sion
sion

    or is it a
    heartbeat

    poem exploding

    unspeakable dimension
    of which only the heartbeat/poem
    is visible

    I see pieces
    go flying
    around an orbit
    zoom back
    like backward-running
    film
    into place

My mother growing
inside me
        holocausts
of freaks
they lead me here
they lead me there

Honest I try
        to be perfect

        Explosion
        of knowledge

        direct hit on the
        experience-dump

        (wherever I go
        I take my *I Ching*
        cheap pocket edition
        electrify all I meet
        with perfect oracles)

        I am so keen
        in my "I"-ness

        the explosions
        are nothing

        preliminary
        props

        nature at work
        perfecting poets

But my virginity!
This is a sad song.
A Greek philosophical song. And I'm
going to sing it in philosophy.

This is the essence
of classical dream.

How could such a monster
have so perfect a voice

the Greek oracles
I would tell all
cannot be classified
refuse miracles:
what will my child be
girl or boy
in the formal

The White Pailomeno

Once there was a beautiful
Pailomeno her name was Lile.
Lile had a trainer and the
trainer liked the horse
very much. One day the
Pailomeno got very very sike
and if the Circus would not
have a horse they would
not have know horse but the
horse was not sike it was
haveing a baby so the circus
was happy and they had two
horses.

A Humpty Dumpty lament.

Death. The Death Kid
a massive view of history!

Fellow citizens, we
are Christ's droppings.

There is a beautiful woman
in my bowels, listen —

struggling to be free

disentangling herself
from my poems.

The Bat People
by Spike Hawkins.

A Beautiful Woman.

(wherever I go
the universe follows
guarding my bowels)

the eggs, cracking!

the poems / the poems

you know / they eat
each other.

Hey there Praxiteles how's that wombman coming?

Or what did you make today?

Poems
>Hey did you see that?
>No what was it?
>Flying saucer!

Marco Polo

If I touch it with my finger my foot hurts.
A secret compound with no name.
To touch it with your tongue is to swallow it.
To swallow it is to die painlessly.
In fact by the expression on his face pleasantly.

The fool was around here yesterday looking for you.
I said here touch your tongue to this

Different poets write from different parts of the body.

For instance, I listened to the radio all day and feel like a new man

"Inflexible purpose"
"Inevitable free will"
"Unconscious universal plan"

"I was dead and am alive!"

"The Ecstasy of not knowing"

"yearning for a mother world"
The Birth of Venus!

"Throat-power. Have a few"
"Edgar Degas (1834–1917)"

"neo-platonic speculation

I do love to watch"
when something happens
in the blankness

something is born
of the sea

feel my nerve hairs
grow big as jugulars

feel the spirit's mouth
yodelling out the universe

(all branches turned
towards the sun —
making syrups)

Feel the power/changes in my body

my body!

body of work

body this green house
wanted to surround

body to which this body that
fetus of electricity
wanted surrounding it.

Rocks of the lower St. Lawrence
Niagara Falls

more exciting than
the fall of man

We used to write
a lot of sonnets
formal bliss

but now don't care
about personalities

everyone's got one
let him use it

the tower
is full of power

love me now

A sonnet, this poet, this man, has, shown, me
shown, me (cough) I, love the way,
life is, really like, that, it was
as if I'd always, known it, and
of, course I, had, although you,
know I, didn't know I, know

Every, day it comes, to, me, I,
(cough) (cough) (COUGH) know,
the inner light, gives, glimpses
that I am a genius, yes,
at base I, know I, know
am so damned, intelligent
I make, dreams, grow,
did, I, think invent me, own

on a borrowed bicycle
I wheel all the way
oh gee if I smashed it
what would he say

he would say I say
there, Archibald
your wife has a bike
and now I have none

you owe me 12 bob
pay up and be gone
I do not like to see
a man with no teeth

did I lose my teeth
in that awful bike smash
or did his fist lash
into my mash
his bike for to crash

Coleridge's shameful lusting
fat little man chasing around
after travel books.

A pleasing whole, entire.
What happened to my head
before I died?

What did it enjoy?

A picture of my poem
chasing after a hundred Coleridges.

I suppose you know
Coleridge was a flute
flute playing a flute

take a trombone
full of water

("She is sensitive
as water"

take a smaller trombone
submerge it into the first
fill that with sand

give love to all
a miracle trombone
in the hand

sweet dove of love above

I want to be of the company of Hemingway, Enigma, Browning,
Poe...
and couldn't write if I didn't consider myself so

there is a man who counts how often certain words
appear in the Holy Bible
                    like "mystery" (28)

                    or "spot-remover" (0)

The (a 2-inch circle of oblivion
        (100 ways to use old Xmas trees
        (a new song offering good wishes
        (a revolution of ideas about history

        perfect Christ that waits for all beings
        even beasts of burden and flesh-eaters

        don't be sad when loved ones die
        it is only the body that falls away
        to be buried in earth or burned to ash

        There, what has happened
        is water freezing
        force us out
        of a dream

        little silkworms of energy
        spinning out bodies

I would spin out poems
like a race civilization

"The book is the last
area of intimacy"

Or the same power
that in me makes this
in darkness makes nature

no question of freedom
chained to eternity
orbit round the sun

to my dearest reader
be you man or woman
hast thou longish hair
touching your neck's base

I am so poorly set

step out into this poem
come into my electrojet

we have awesome powers
have grown out of our sex

have known the sun and moon
named constellations

talked ourselves
into idiocy

words are for burning!

a point of light
living in flames

What I do not say
listen only to that
my love

Today and every day
I try to please
the dead,

in observation
of my bewildering
freedom / chains

Mother, here's a little poem —
for when time gives me up

an excellent universe you are!
an excellent mother you are
excellent daughter
poem, or

I don't know what you are!
but I spring from you
you spring from me

glimpses of you dreaming
inside the flames

— my love

My body.   The absolute poem
is flesh.   Soon I'll be
silent.

        the receptacle aspect
        of the human form

        A reconstruction
        on the book plane

        of a simple dream
        formed, forever altered

        by my desires
        so complex

        desires, springing
        from my precepts.

        The dream is simple,
        transcends numbers

                        December 28, 1966
                        to February 20, 1967,
                        Hamilton, Ontario.

The Ova Yogas

being a series of poems
written in one long
strange afternoon

The Warm Rain

It was so warm today
and felt like rain,
started to rain about 4

and old man Whitlaw telling
of sparrows in his attic —
They are only sparrows
says he, not eagles.

And he had me feel
his arm, the muscle
all melted away.

I am ten years younger
than Bertrand Russell
he said, and my muscles
all melting away.

The Combination

The holy work
of our lives

touching
Easter Island,
the human stones.

*

Isla de Pascua.

Come, see the place
where the Lord lay.

*

The sky opens
like a flower

when the stone
is placed.

My Personal

My personal Grand Canyon:
the page, my word —
yodelling across it;

this no limit
to what I can say
and so much I can't.

So much I can't say
I'm crushed by what
I can and can't say—

Oh canyon of death,
what I can and can't
say are the same.

The Buzz

Three fingers zipt
(off) (or on) (or
off and on)

No pain at first.

Happy happy happy
cutting lumber,
building a garage

zip

sad sad sad.

Elaphent

The pwam, for ward
on the comniccwasmwas

Head for the pwam
it is the centaur

absolid infwamation

wear the day
becalms impwassibly

Vision

People plor compless
magniphalce
p'tout

cryin boost
f'my hat.

tlast mavisions
makzens.

Cec Busy

Krasple'rt a kavis-
ing bliss? Cec busy

zith blep-belp, qu!
Terranspoil of agle,
agle-ova Manitoba.

Awant agle agen.

Kib? Iysleval kib
a kevis agle agen.

Belp-belb (plep-belp)
Manitoba kib agle
kib terrans bliss.

Bliss awant ova.

(Agle-ova ib of.)

Worgen-Weight

Til'm-worgen aden
A budd niss amy
tawit: A. *Tawit*

Flim-worgen, Oh—

Friday amy, f
wafter-wave

   (fF is fef)

Wo'gen distry
Oliver World!

Nervispring

Unthirsty asputi
fallspring ego
wole canmelti sno

woldenmen blown
snottispitti slop

nervispring assing
ano adieu ago

getmi tefus wet
enmudsno misho Oh
full lip art

metaphor agolden
asshole shodo

Treebarkall

Wignet t i t

p p p p p

o! o! o! o! o!

Dichez hay
devfing lifs

Sum Or

NWT pea
pill

numba shtreeee

I sno

We Cake

& trumpt
inthend

bloobymis

o lisn
lisn

the son.

Miles

Miles
yawds'n
feat, y'no

rising do
rhizome

in chis
lite cheers

hill indials
my dolawkz

frever fever

Owes along
w'ay

Vermeer/Turner
awain

Awnin awnin,
thessa lonely
pig, high err

o thessa
prickleback
(Scuvian bird)

O Lesco
slover
thistle

thartmus
knobby strande.

Ova miles
miles

fleshland
m'm'm.

Abby Deaf

Innering.
Bro. bible
— a durn.

Blim baaw
sibyl.

Sable, coff.
We all (y)
here

tribleding
abby leaf.

Spim

Ardis heart.
Indies lessian

spim?

Wear I come from
is no wore

blood'n muscle
frenz

Done fill bad!
Ass, assori.

Thendle Gowen Growing

Wormth, try
on fabulls, ball

you manwill
ova quikt

ova, ova
ova,

    nome
prum dilt,
adilt, wormtry
ball spire

No!

Threem adith
mature, natur

wee woodna no
sproust…

afraid?
otha drifting
ova sentries

untamother
no their
ovacomings

O sdream!

Hive, come —
I'll ova!

Gowen
(many)

Endsil

Uplane drones
Marshafter nuins

collet.

   "But
tunes, milky
enhermio kney"
(tear fix
smoke lune)

this kigh
sociaigh.

Spurt Hill
1968

Hollow

Wee, it mums.
Oh, on end on,
tharrel bino
(bino's wun)
uptul sun

lippskull

enlip d'yore

enlip, it
smems end
smems or...?

Nou?
(ab bri)

Frilshi, bellomero
planet, bellomero

frost awliddie
promise lost,
regamed —

forsh of forsh,
blendend!

Theer Jief Bailed
("Nou Yeed Telp," Houth Yold)

Mich, mich nuppen trob (be).
No menting alloved,
not achur H.

Spittle nip pinnon spo
who spun ander durd
"PEACE," andigger, oil
ops kind of ips,
if melisso.

Homeris om eric
Egypturd,

"stuffis love,
stuffis love."

I, Reco, mmend
you, twice-barled

inn *wife*
or durd

butt dool:
frihum dum nit
your children
your weerk,
groan't ssume —

Why? aromo,
arom bitter
of speed,
trez er
omo, opo.

Ellling, om
ingor ellom
sputi fall,

aster.

1972

The Poet's Progress

For Doug, Gerry, Vic D'Or,
Snorri Thordarsson,
the poets of the 21st century
and the women at No. 9

"Consider the lives of birds and fishes. Fish never weary of the water; but you do not know the true mind of a fish, for you are not a fish. Birds never tire of the woods; but you do not know their real spirit, for you are not a bird. It is just the same with the religious, the poetical life: if you do not live it, you know nothing about it."
— R. H. Blyth

"All the twists and turns of character of which we are so proud are perhaps, at bottom, impersonal."
— Eugen Herrigel

I

What did the sun say to the earth?
You can't go home again.

I don't know where I am
or how I got here, lost
among the water-logged logs
in a warm sunless swamp.

The crows are all around me —

Suddenly, the sound of traffic
and I'm slicing a tomato,

the windows are at rest,
full of trust,

a small dog looks at me,
its tail wagging —

Poetry makes me fall awake,
see myself a part of it,

no longer forced to pick the pear
before ripeness is there,

the greed of a spoiled child of thirty-four
who has not learned what fruit is for —

II

In the giant weekend crossword puzzle
I put LABORERS instead of ASPIRERS
for the clue *Ambitious people*

which delayed my solution 15 minutes
and cut into my working time,

time I could have spent aspiring
to a magical life free of pain,
time I could have spent staring
into the pain of the orbiting earth,
challenging it to engulf me,
a bloated ant planning, aspiring
for a perfect death among the other ants

and my children have burnt the toast
and are excitedly trying to waft the smoke
out the open door

into the falling sun

into a storm of light,

four loaves of lovely bread
rising in the oven.

And at 2 a.m. I drink
the last of the wine,
memories of you continue
to lie in me like dregs.

I watch the rain
on the window
then take a shower
then return to the gleaming
paper, this smooth expensive
pen I found on the street,

memories of the wine goblet
sitting on the paper
casting a shadow across it.

I took off my boots
and found a small piece
of black electrical tape
stuck to the sole of one of them,
I could not remember
where I could have picked it up,

my mind went soaring
back over the past ten hours
trying to remember
and failed,

and the paper is as white
as a window into heaven

and the words I write on it
are full of eternal significance,
profound emptiness,
planets encircling a sun
forever, casting
sharp little shadows
into my frightened eyes

for the world will never stop
its ear-splitting raids on heaven.
Gerry would never have written that,
Gerry only raising his voice
to ask to be left alone

with naked heaven
in his gentle arms.

And Vic D'Or in the golden light
flicks his forked tongue
and frowns and stretches.

He tells of how it all
(started) (ended)
with him —

an accident! It was
an ordinary day in the lab

and someone left the room,
the wind knocked over a retort,
a red-hot tuning fork
seared a notebook
and within moments the whole room
was engulfed in strange verse.

The poet is a token
of the world's magic,
heaven is a fiery field
of endless energy
and will swamp the world
at the flick of a
forked switch —

III

I was sitting in the garden
admiring the apple blossoms,
a high wind came up and one by one
the blossoms broke from their boughs
and blew away
                        until each bough
was bare of beauty,

the blossoms' little eyes full of tears
bidding me adieu,
                        and by habit
lines composed themselves in my head
striving to express the moment's essence.

And for the past month of bursting spring
my lines have become full of my mind
that cramped tomb of dying light

as if someone had whispered to me
in a dream I'd forgotten
there's much in there that shouldn't
remain unexamined

after so many effortless
years of writing
                        thousands of lines
whose worth it would be well to doubt,
in a life of silence letting the lines
slowly sprout from the tongue like leaves

and perhaps at that point I entered
the irreversible second
half of my life
                    where what
was ignored in the first becomes
dominant, what was crucial
in the first dies
like an insignificant dream.

My tome, my time is running out.
Let me clear out this smelly tomb
and discover what's behind it.

And the lines ignored those other blossoms
that blossomed in my mind then blew away
blossoms posing complex questions such as
how many springs will I enjoy before I die,
questions that can't be ignored in verse
that strives to capture the moment's essence

questions embarrassing as adolescent poems
but no more embarrassing than the blossoms

so ridiculously beautiful,
and as essential as the moment's
essence

but the vanishing blossoms were closer
than my thoughts and far more innocent

and remain so even though they're gone
and will be long again after I'm gone,

my existence dependent on my admiration
of you and I admired you

as you unfolded your small white petals
with the same gentle force that opens
my small white eyelids and lets
the lines sprout from my lips
and I admired you as you were blown away
by the same wind that wears me out,

the lips part and another line pops out,

the incompleteness of my existence
failing as I have to admire
the tree that gave you your brief lives
in exchange for your brief lives

and the small clouds that made
brief shadows on my silken face
as one by one you vanished,

the trees all around me shuddering in the wind
like giant voluptuous bass violins
and the air all around me full
of vanishing blossoms and I
didn't shudder in the wind,
didn't vanish, disappear.

For when you are with me you speak
an unknown language closer
to me than my mother's tongue
and I love to hear you babble
with pleasure like a river
flowing back through time
as you do when I give myself
to your embrace —

and I can't help believing you
when you say you'll always return.

I don't care how foolish I appear
for there is nothing I can hide from you,
can I become the man you'll never leave?

You've been everywhere, seen everything
and your embrace is like an infant's
starving for my essential juices

and you give me the power
to see into all mysteries
but your own

and we are forever parting
before our embrace exhausts us —

you disappear on a cloud of sperm cells
leaving me as weak as a man can be

and in an hour I'm strong
and have forgotten you in the beauty
of the Eden you've illuminated

and in the moment of greatest light
you return full of darkness and love

and everything you give me I squander
and I can't help trusting you
when you say you'll always return.

IV

I'm unable to speak ill of you
but I want to die when you are gone,
the arrogance of a man unable to accept
his inability to understand
the cosmos, a blade of grass.
And the fear that comes with not knowing
when you'll return is only dispelled
by being engulfed by it,

and as I stopped at a red light,
no traffic anywhere, three in the morning,
downtown Hamilton Ontario, the voice
of a network disc jockey from Vancouver
saying "God bless jazz fans everywhere,"

and as I drove along the streets of night
icy spirits floated along beside the car
staring in at me with innocent curiosity
and at almost every block fresh streams
of mournful memories were triggered —
foolish memories belying the complexity
of the sacred moment, memories
that were mine alone
                              unlike the moment
which belongs to the point on which I stand,
and the icy spirits, human, but of an unidentifiable
racial origin, were merely watching
as a hen might watch an egg —

V

And we return to ancient times,
to an unrecorded history,
an inconceivable richness
that whistles through our hearts,

and all poets know they live
in ancient times
and with the cold eye of the future
view the glory of their lives —

With one foot in the grave
and the other in the womb, they view
the gentle drift of continents,
phases of the endless psyche —

All that is not easily measured
is out of place in this century
and the human race was born yesterday
and will die tomorrow

and a man carrying a crooked stick
along a city street is an omen of destruction,
each step he takes is a technological advance,
each step he takes is a step into hell,

cursed with an inability to love,
an unwillingness to accept that we
can never know our warm, leafy
surroundings but can only be them.

And proud of her new radio, my little girl
was listening to a Christmas concert.

They played Puff, the Magic Dragon
and she cried.
                    She began cutting
some paper with a pair of scissors.
She picked up her doll, it was
about four inches tall, made from dried
corn husks, it had a small red book
in its hands, it had brown hair
with two tiny red ribbons.

I wonder who made this doll, she said,
and what they're doing right now.
And then she said, *Maybe*
they're making another doll.

I had a pack of cards and began teaching
the little girl to play solitaire.
Suddenly I no longer believed I was there
teaching the little girl to play solitaire,
I believed I was somewhere else, in the future,
remembering the time I taught
the little girl to play solitaire,

or as Juvenal put it in his *Tenth Satire,*
On the Vanity of Human Wishes: "Many perished
who trusted overmuch in their muscles"
and all the streets are clogged
with shiny American cars
and all the cars are clogged
with decaying Canadian meat,

or as John Bunyan put it in his
Pilgrim's Progress, "For it is happened
to him according to the true proverb,
the dog is turned to his vomit again

and the sow that was washed to her
wallowing in the mire."

      Dear friend,
I usually keep my door unlocked
but if for any reason you find it locked
the key is in this poem.

And he gave me chapter two of his
pornographic novel to read
so I read it and gave him my latest
purest poem to look at

and he read it out to his wife
and several others who happened
to be in the room and he made
several humorous changes
as he went along

and so I read his chapter aloud
inserting his wife's name
for the name of his porno queen

and after a few pages
of steadily increasing tension
she stormed out of the house
vowing never to return —

VI

The old poet in the black overcoat
stood at the side of the road
watching workmen take down
a dead willow. He was trying

to determine the size of the tree
at various periods of his life
and the lives of others, trying
to determine at which point certain
poems were written.

He thought of his children.

One was a 47-year-old Manpower
counsellor, unmarried. The other
committed suicide at 28, an event
that prevented him from writing poems
for several weeks. No grandchildren.
He regretted never having written
for his children when they were small.

There was a certain pleasure
in these painful thoughts
for they reminded him
he wasn't senile
although he could not remember
the tree before today, strange
because he lived in this
neighbourhood all his life,
nor was he the possessor
of the legendary wisdom of the aged.

He indulged in these painful thoughts
on an irregular and unplanned basis.
These painful thoughts came to him
when they were needed
like a tornado, earthquake
or volcanic eruption, none of which
he had experienced in the flesh.

They were neither good nor bad
but a reminder of eternal nature,
laughably. It would be
several days before they returned.
In the interim his mind
was a clear tropical sky,
the sun moving across it,
the smell of blossoms,
lazy bird rhythms.

During these periods he regarded
the phases of his life
as the phases of the moon, or
as layers of sediment left behind
by prehistoric seas,
the dates being the subject
of endless academic argument,
the layers hardened far beyond
amusement or regret.

His house was built on the brow
of the Niagara Escarpment and he could see
the layers in his mind
and all around the neighbourhood.
Death would be a disappointment.
The rocks would soften and dissolve.

It was no different than the community
of chess players or the community
of insurance salesmen I argued
although of course without conviction.
I had gone too long without sleep.
What was I doing here?
His eyes never blinked. He looked
at me as if watching dancing flames.

I felt burnt out, my guts stuffed
with cold indigestible food.
This was always happening to me.
Paintings from the 1920s
hung on the wall.
I couldn't identify them
although they seemed familiar.
He told me he keeps a loaded gun
under his bed and writes at his best
during periods of paranoia.
I told him I'm afraid of guns
because of frequent bouts of erotomania
brief but intense during which
I could easily do myself in
and the likelihood would increase
with loaded guns lying all around.
I told him I only write when uninspired.
His wife told me that after all these years
they're still frequently on the verge
of breaking up.
She is particularly annoyed when he
prowls around the house late at night
with the gun in his hand
after the last late show goes off.

She also resents the time he spends
on the telephone with his sister,
lengthy long distance calls after midnight,
and his wife's eyes and my eyes met
and we seemed to share a wave
of inexpressible envy for his sister.

And she was lying in bed reading
a book about Evelyn Dick, the famous
Hamilton murderess of the 1940s

and she said it irks her that convicted
murderers are living among us
after having served their time,
free to watch the trees
blossom in the spring,
free to gaze into the heavens
in all their glorious moods,
free to go shopping
and order choice cuts of meat

while those they have murdered
lie rotting in the ground

and I do not want to argue with her
for fear one of us will end up dead —

and later in the cold rain
I came around the corner
on the new bicycle
and saw her excited face
looking out the window —

it was her birthday,
the bicycle was for her —

VII

With its four bare branches
the tree resembled a football player
kicking a perfect punt,
the sun burning his outstretched fingers.

A swing swung from one of the branches,
I thought a little girl had put it up
for the ropes were tied to the branch
with little pink bows.

In the garden by the tree were three
tulips, one yellow and two red.
There were also two giant sunflowers, one
as tall as the tree, the other slightly less.

The grass surrounding the garden
was darker than the leaves of the tree,
the blue of the sky was a peculiar tone
that didn't fade toward the horizon.

Each sunflower had four leaves,
each tulip two. Fourteen altogether.

VIII

Were they gulls or merely teardrops
in the angry sky strangling the sun?
Were they rabbits on a black bald cliff?

Below the cliff was a softly pointed
green hill with little roses growing
around the peak.

On the top of the hill
was a lovely rose tree
with ten blossoms in full bloom
each branch stretching out to the
drowning sun.

The rabbits on closer inspection
became swans.

IX

With its three stubby branches
the tree resembled a three-fingered hand
beckoning someone away from the flowers
and sheltering a weak tree of roses
with six blossoms.
A rusty old shovel that looked
as if it had just been placed there
rested against the tree. *Which tree?*
The tree with three stubby branches.
Flowers. There were four flowering plants,
each bearing one flower:
of the two small plants one bore a yellow
flower and the other an orange flower,
and of the two large plants one bore a
yellow flower and the other an orange.
In each case the plant bearing the orange
flower was slightly taller than the one
bearing the yellow flower, and the shortest
yellow-flowered plant was the same
height as the tree of roses.

A man in a purple suit, green shoes
and yellow gloves walked out of eight
into nine and as he did his suit
turned mauve and his shoes violet.

The two large plants each had four leaves,
the two small ones each had two
for a total of twelve.

X

The tree looked like a bird with two heads
with its four upthrust branches
full of green leaves and red apples.
There were seven apples.
An eighth was falling
into a bushel already full.
There was a cute little swing
attached to the branch of the tree.

XI

With its tiny zigzag branches
the tree looked like lightning,
the green leaf halo a
noxious gas it emits.

At its base two red petunias
seemed about to vomit
while a pair of prudish marigolds
waited patiently and hoped
they wouldn't be splattered.

On a soft rounded green hill
or was it the sky's rancid
eyeball drooping
there was a small rose tree
with six yellow blossoms
burning in the rays of the sun.

XII

And the years have been tough on her
but she is tougher than the years,
more awful than time itself.
And she is tougher than I've ever been
and knows more of heaven and hell
than any twelve poets you could name.
I'm always naked in her eyes
and full of weaknesses
that bring no smile of compassion.

I think of other men years ago
she could have paired with
and she knows I was not the best
but only the most persistent.
Her sensitivity and immediacy
leave me in an agony of envy
and we're bonded in natural love
with time and children
and endless work.

I think of the child she was
and the demands I have placed on her
that have crushed her and made another,
how my life has devoured hers
and my shifting despairs
have forced her to take stands
in opposition to me, actual steps
away from me —

How well do I know her?
We stand for every pair of opposites
the Fall invented —
How well does darkness know light?

And she has taken on an immensity
that alters everything I see
but doesn't alter me

as I stand directly between her
and the sky
casting ugly shadows on her face.

She cries quietly and swallows her tears.
Her hands are like the roots of an oak.

She says she is happy with me
and I make a crack about her mother.

Her daughters look at me in sorrow
and vow never to marry.

She tells me I have upset her.
I feel putrid, she says.

She says she's going out in the car.
I tell her to drive carefully.
I know how to drive, she says.

I'm not a moron, she says.
*I'm not a child, you treat
me like you treat the kids.*

And she notes with perfect accuracy
the people I criticize for exploiting her
exploit her far less than I do

and the most ghastly cut of all —
is there a poet who has never
felt these lovely words
caressing his tears: *You think
your poems are more important than life itself!*

One fine poet I know
was so shattered by a remark
      like that from his wife
he couldn't write for months
and began moaning about the
vanity and triviality of it all —

And the sorrow she felt for the poet N.
when his wife killed herself,
was it the same as my genuine sorrow
or were there subtle differences
I failed to comprehend?

And I know how arrogant it sounds
when I say it's been a good marriage
and for a moment I consider
drastic remedial measures
say a thirty-day fast
as penance for having destroyed her

and I am powerless to complain
about the destruction of this country
when I have personally and slowly
over a deathless decade
destroyed one of this country's

finest flowers
and yet being human she flowers
daily
        and oh my God she's still talking
talking talking talking,
my wife silent and the woman
on the TV droning on
in a dishonest drawl

while I look at the floor, the shoes
on the floor full of envy.

XIII

There are colours I cannot name,
there is one now
hanging from the ceiling.

I can't describe the tie
hanging from the doorknob,

the door slightly ajar
and a red sweater
extending from the closet's darkness
like a tongue —

What is that unearthly
glorious light? Is it part
of Mecca's Sacred Shrine? No,
it is the sewing machine, my wife
silent and the woman
forgot to shut it off —

There are other things in this room.
There is me for instance.
There is Jesus, Joseph and Mary
hanging on the wall, Mary is gazing
at Jesus, and Joseph is trying to peer
down Mary's dress, and there is the sound
of the TV where a man is reciting this poem.

There is a book on pyramids.
There is a bicycle. There is a
red hanky I could tell a funny
story about and probably will
after this poem is finished.

There is something I can't quite
put my finger on. No,
that left the room
as soon as I mentioned it
even though I didn't mention it.

Each word as I write it
comes into this room.
Perhaps somewhere in some
other room these very words
are disappearing, this poem
being unwritten, losing
a word at a time
quickly then slowly
at varying speeds
from end to beginning —

A chair is here
right where the last person
to touch it put it
unless the cat which is

not in this room but
has been
brushed against it with
enough force to move it
into its present position
from its past position
(and everything she says
has six or seven meanings,
all of them painful)
but that is not likely
since it's a heavy chair
and a light cat
too sensible to waste
energy moving this chair
that is not here
(these words are here)
and has been moved
many times
and in each place it's been
it has stayed for varying
lengths of time
perhaps as much as ten years
in one spot at one time
since it is an old chair.

It moved!
Not by itself although it
would be possible
to write that
but rather someone
came into the room
and moved it
the chair not the room
slightly then
went out too fast

for me to see but I see
the chair has been moved
slightly.

What colour is the chair?
It is a sandy shade but
smoother, reflecting
the light from the sacred
sewing machine.

It is the colour of pine
smoothly sanded
once growing in a
Nova Scotia forest.

The chair is there.
The words are here.
I am here, there
and everywhere, a poem
that can only be defined
by other poems, a focus
of nature's benevolence,
hostility, that can only
be located by others.

There is a bottle of beer
in this room but there
is no bottle.
The beer is inside me,
the empty bottle is
outside me
and this room
but inside another
room
and inside a case

of other bottles
some capped and containing
beer and some empty
like I will be after the beer
is no longer inside me.

Please beer with me.

There is hair in this room.
It is on various parts
of my body's surface
growing out of it,
rooted into it
like tiny trees in
a Nova Scotia forest.

XIV

A mind
is at work
in this room
is this true?

I have no way of knowing
nor of judging
the words that are
here and here and here
as well as there and
neither here nor there yet
or should I have written
yet
on a separate line?

The word, each word,
each comma, comes
out of the pen that is
in my hand like a
gun, something called
the mind a sort of trigger

a dishonest drawl

firing blind shots
at unseen future events.

Am I being honest
or dishonest? Am I
fulfilling my destiny?
Am I preparing to
meet my doom?

Doom, perhaps this
is a doom room,
this room my doom,
this room I see being
a room inside a larger
field of space in which
a moon is hung.

Who hung the moon?
Did the cat brush
against it? If it
did it would not know
it did but did it
without knowing it?

I could put a number
here:

XV

And then I could put
a number
here:

XVI

This is the sixteenth part.
The sixteenth part is here!
Come in, sixteenth part.

Hello, my name is Constant Arousal.
I am the sixteenth part.
I am the smoking cigarette
which, along with other cigarettes,
has been in this room for
many hours. I do not
care about my health,
just these words.

This is my bedroom.
This room of doom
is my bedroom
where I sleep.

Sometimes there are
dreams in this room!

But more often merely
awful infinity.

The sound of a car
is in this room
as these words appear
but no car sound
is in this room
as these words appear.

A car went by on a
street within earshot
a short time ago
and I *predict*
another will come by
soon and the sound.

There is a list of complaints
in this room. They are
not in words. They are
in a wordless list
in a listless mind
in a semi-broken
body in this room.

My body is scarred
and is not healthy
although it is healthier
than other bodies
at least in theory.

Should the list
appear on this page?

I have no complaints
about this room.
It is good enough
for me and I for it.

An I for an I.
It is good enough
for God,
foreign eye.

There is happiness
in this room.
There is a chair.
There is light.
There is sound.

I do not feel up to
describing the sounds
in this room.

I have only now noticed
that as I write I say
the words, whisper them
as I write them.

And a child in another
room within earshot
took one sudden deep breath
among a lifetime
of relatively
shallow breaths

and I only now noticed
that I myself am breathing
my breathing
made irregular
by the words I am
whispering as I write.
Right? As I write them.

I *predict* I will
someday type
out these words
in another room
on more suitable paper

but to *predict*
is not as pleasant
as to write words

for the happiness
in this room
is relative
to the words I write
rather than the words
I predict

and I suppose I feel
a sense of responsibility
for the happiness in this room,
the chair that is there
and will be there
in that position
for an undetermined
length of time about which
I will make no predictions.

Chair. The happiness
in this room will remain
until it is moved, a motion.

The Holy Family
hovers above the chair
and shares in the chair's
happiness

although it contributes
less holiness
than the sewing machine
and less happiness
than the writing
of these words.

There is pain
in this room, specifically
in a tooth in my jaw,
a bad tooth that was
not always bad
but will have to go
for detracting however
slightly from the
happiness in this room,
and that's the tooth!

And now

IV

that list of complaints:

Our language has too
many words. Words I
could destroy include
heaven
holiness
happiness
food poisoning

in fact every word
but the word I am
at this moment
writing, whispering.

Here is my second complaint:
I have no more complaints

except that I have never
written a word about which
I had no complaints

but I think it is time
to correct that.

VOMIT

I have now written a word
about which I have
no complaints.

Which word is that?
The word is

VOMIT

A healthy mind in a
healthy room.

There's a lot of health
in the old mind yet
but it doesn't turn over
the way it used to.

You should be able to see
a poet's mind turning over,
you should be able to know
what he is thinking at all times
even when he is vomiting
even when he is in a drunken
shouting match with a guy
who has been sitting in a
Chinese restaurant in Collingwood
for seven years waiting for him
to show up

and he said *I don't think you're man
enough* and the next day Doug said
*I thought he said I don't think you're
mad enough!*

And the mind is becoming
more and more
like the chair there
steadfast as a star
radiant as a chair
or at least
the chair there.

I am where I am.

I am chair, I am.

I am the light
from the sewing machine
and the way
of all words.

I went around the word
in eighty ways.

A memory: .
Yesterday I saw a
pretty postperson prancing
in the park.

She took off all her
predictions.

The grass turned into a colour
I don't feel up to describing.

A stream began to flow
where before
there had been
no stream

but it was no surprise.

She took my hand
and placed it
between the sun and the moon

and the stream
began to flow.

And so

XVIII, XIX & XX

After the poem left the room
and began to indulge in memory
creating a decidedly artificial tone

I put my head on a pillow
and fell asleep,

woke up a few hours later
with intense stomach pains.

Took a few codeine tablets
I'd had following removal
of a mess of rotting teeth.

Now I am pleasantly
floating and these words
are coming too fast
although I am sincerely
trying not to let on
the words are coming too fast.

While I slept I thought
about this poem and developed
a marvellous end technique
that not only resolved this piece
but resolved problems I've been
trying to vocalize all my life
and I knew that finally
everyone would understand me

even Doug, Gerry, Vic D'Or
and the women at No. 9.

Then the pains came
destroying all that delicacy
and in my present pleasant
mood I'm not going to strain
to bring it back.

For perfect stress
avoid rest —

XXI

What if my left thumb
suddenly fell off?

XXII

When the dentist left the room
my hand went up his nurse's skirt.
When he came back he broke my tooth
then spent an hour rooting for the root

kneeling on the arms of my chair
if not my own arms or the arms
I laughingly call my own
because no one else wants them
or if they do they don't tell me
because they're too shy
but no one should be shy
life being as short as it is —
each cautious moment cuts a life in half
until there's nothing left —

And that was either yesterday or tomorrow
and during the writing of this poem
I've tried to be honest and sincere
as well as dishonest and insincere

and my appetite has returned.

Mount Hamilton, Ontario
1974–1976

I Don't Know

Emperor Wu of Liang: Who are you to stand before us like this?
Bodhidharma: I don't know.

I

At midnight at forty below the North Bay bus terminal
becomes a stately pleasure dome, the beauty of its steaming
warmth brings tears to my frozen eyes. And then silence,
the ticket agent breathing softly, my heart somewhere beating
and off in the distance a bus crunching through the hard snow
like a finger moving over velvet, and oh!
that sunny pleasure dome with caves of ice.

And the buses, pointing in all directions,
long enclosed chariots full of ancient Franks and Druids
and the occasional Abyssinian maid
drinking the milk of paradise,
wingless whining airliners with blinking lights,
where have they come from, where are they going
and what rich incalculable dreams do they contain,
what soft dullness, what shafts of ecstasy at play?

"Pensez-vous que je suis stupide?" he asked.
The girl looked confused and said, "Pourquoi?"
"Parce-que je suis anglais. Dans les films québécois
les anglais sont toujours stupides."
Her answer was a warm embrace,
soft and blushing with new love.

Suddenly she discovered her watch had stopped
and the midnight bus to Montreal had left.
Perhaps they would be spending another night together
or would it be their first?

But the ticket agent, crazed with compassion,
ran out into the frozen road in urgent shirtsleeves
and flagged down a giant turtle of a bus,

its shell caked with caves of ice and snow,
its windows a row of black intelligent stones.

And the poor girl couldn't find the key
to the locker where her luggage was stored,
she and the boy frantically going through their pockets
full of junk, the boy with less enthusiasm, shyly
hoping she would be forced to stay another night
and the bus sitting there like a rocketship
after the final countdown. Would it blast off
and when? The fates bounced around the steaming
pleasure dome like velvet bolts of lightning
searching for a key.

A long poem begins when a poet accepts his ignorance
and moves out into all the magic space he can afford
with longing for the capture of a moment so perfect
all moments will submit forever to his will.
But it must be an act of gentleness,
no strain must be apparent
for the moments that beat like invisible hearts
are sensitive animals who despise clumsiness
and when a poet becomes softer than those moments
and more sensitive, a small poem can appear
like a huge miracle …

Before a long poem
a poet can only stand in stupid ignorance,
knowing only kindness must be shown to words,
his mindlessness steeped in a simple divinity.
Poetry is a man sitting alone in a room
with a ticking clock, the poet the mere tip
of an ancient pyramid. He's only
the tip of a pyramid, sitting alone in a room
perched atop a mile-high cone of human bones.

Poetry is merely a man supported by a lonely room,
an invisible pyramid of loving flesh
that cuts through the centuries if you care to descend,
for poetry is flesh cutting through the sharpest knife.
And the unfulfilled dead may tear at your heart
but the dead poets will caress you,
and their unwritten lines belong to you
as much as the hairs of your lovely head —
belonging to you in the sense of constantly offered,
great riches lying in some unopened room
of an old despised house.

Did she find the key? Did the bus
finally leave without her, leave her to spend
another final night in his arms? Did Quebec
come to peace with Canada, at rest
like the vision of a silly poet, his flesh
engorged with language?

II

For it does not befit a man
to worry overmuch about his verse.

And that which is studied starts to stink
and the ultimate stink is the stench
of one who strives for perfection

and evil ultimately rests
on sound and light and movement
and what can be more boring than an
artist defending his chosen themes?

But there are certain utterances
that just burst out, come yelping helplessly
from unseen personal cavernous harmonies,
from foolish wombs,

utterances so mysterious, perfect and mellifluous
they embarrass the cautious guardians of literature
whose eyes narrow as they question
the relevance of such personal data

and you have not written anything worthwhile
until you have seen them turn away
in carefully concealed confusion

for the ones from whose wombs burst the bitches of rhyme
are the ones who burn with joy and personal terror

and they are condemned to contemplate endlessly
the particular forms of the flames that consume them.

III

Who is sleeping and who is not,
who is dreaming holy and enchanted dreams
and who is at the toilet, vomiting,
in this little city to my left?

It's Rivière-du-Loup in its pre-dawn lights,
the sleeping St. Lawrence River
moving slowly around it like a lover's arm,
meandering with a lazy motion

and on my right as I race along this dreamlike road
from Kingston to Edmundston

are the Gaspé hills over which
the sun is ready to raise its endlessly burning staff,
and the grey trees like frozen wisps of smoke
are ready to melt.

Where is my soul? Not in those lights
nor in that sky of lost glory.
It has sunk through caverns measureless to man
down to a sunless sea no human thought has touched,

and perhaps a few in that little city
are listening to the same radio station,
the only one I can get in the Franco-American night,
some all-night U.S. phone-in show
where people call from all over the hemisphere,
including, as the announcer says, Greenland,
Newfoundland, Nova Scotia and Hawaii.

And someone from San Francisco calls to complain
about how long it took him to get through
and when he finishes complaining he says he called
to say he'd just finished eating a piece of cake.

"Oh? What kind of cake?" asks the kindly announcer.
"Spice cake," says the San Franciscan. "It was good."

And a flutter of little invisible smiles from the
lights of Rivière-du-Loup monotonously
ache their way up into the sentimental sky and disappear,
Rivière-du-Loup suddenly I recall was the same town
where almost twenty years ago I got off the train
and bought an ice cream cone from a pretty girl
who made an ugly remark and gave me a frozen stare
along with the ice cream, possibly, as I later sadly thought,
because I had neglected to speak *en français*.

And the girl, is she somewhere among those lights,
two decades later, listening to this radio program,
but more probably sleeping, has she changed much,
does she still have unconscious molecules of my heart
under her fingernails?

And there was a stone wolf carved on the side of the bridge
but I must maintain my schedule, and cannot afford
to drive into town to see if it is still there
and if the bridge has been ripped out
and replaced by a wider one
and if the ice cream shop has been ripped out
and replaced by a Holiday Inn
I do not want to know.

IV

And the confidence to begin a new piece of writing
comes of having no other confidence worth mentioning,
it's enough that I'm alive among the flames
and a moment ago casually washed
the blood from my hands.

What interests me is this writing. The blood
was merely from another in a long line of dead cows.
Like most people obsessed with the mysteries
of language murder is something I shy away from
although I've been known to strike out in fury,
invariably missing my target, striking out,
as if with purpose, my fury never totally blind.

Many poets have killed themselves.
Some have killed others.
Even more have been murdered
among the flames.

And today I spent two hours in a hot bath
listening to the icicles fall from the eaves

while my wife was in Port Dover
going through the business of buying a carcass of beef
for our new freezer which arrived two days ago
on the coldest day of the year. I pushed open
the frosty door and a man covered with snow
said your freezer is here.

Today, fresh from the bath, the whole city melting,
I was met at the door with boxes and boxes of meat
freshly killed, my wife saying I'll bring it in,
you'll catch cold fresh from the bath.
We sorted the various cuts into plastic bags
and the blood was thicker than I imagined.

And now as these lines break into time
the cuts of meat slowly lose their warmth
and the new freezer purrs with electric life,
and for a moment I suck my lip where I cut myself
while shaving

and there are cattle spotted all over
the vast warm land masses of this globe,
grazing, mating, giving birth. They cringe
from blizzards, seek shade in heat,
drink when thirsty, sleep when tired

and it seems likely they never compose verse
although I'm sure mental shapes, horny images,
glisten in their bovine dreams

and at times they become confused, even frantic,
as they somehow sense their horrendous fate

and it seems likely one need not be human
to experience visions of angels at critical moments

and I say from the depths of my folly
it seems likely it's merely a matter
of being central to vast dying lovelinesses.

V

And the sky over Hamilton comes into awesome view
as the bus threads its way up through layers of ancient rock
reminding me the city is observable from the air,
is located in a dimension that permits charting,
exists on a plane with other cities,
this city I've lived in so long,
this city I don't know.

A hundred crows hang in the air like suspended
particles of soot, they are so far away,
softly fluttering particles of soot
hanging in the haze over the bayfront
the sky in the late afternoon of colour,
unnamable blends of vibrating colour,
long slanting beams of light
poor humans try in vain to paint

and the eyes of others on the bus
are filled with the awful colours of the sky
and every earlobe is tinged with pink

and suddenly the crows turn eastward and fly
rapidly out of view, and a woman gets on the bus
carrying a book entitled *Courage of the Morning*,
and I think of poor Dick Cunningham, whose feet
have just been amputated.

VI

She was cutting trees in the Scottish Highlands
in the latter years of the Second World War
and Tom Parsons was on leave from the Cameron Highlanders of
Ottawa
and he was on his way to visit relatives in the Orkneys
and they met by accident in Edinburgh.
                                    "Oh, you could write
a lovely story about our romance," she said
as she sat by the Cenotaph in Hamilton Ontario
thirty-two years later. Tom was marching in the Remembrance Day
Parade
and I looked at the clock outside the newspaper office
and it was 10:55 and my program said four restored fighter planes
were due to fly overhead — two Harvards, a Corsair and a Mustang
P-51 —
but it was too foggy.
                    "Same thing as last year,
same kinda day exactly. Only a quarter-mile visibility
but we'll try again next year," said the guy at the airport.

The six old women sat on the green bench as the service continued,
huddled in their winter coats, their silver crosses, slightly tarnished,
fastened to their lapels. They were the
Silver Cross Mothers of Hamilton, whose sons were killed in the
wars.

"Victor was a dear little fellow," she said.
"I often wonder what his life would have been like.
His older brothers were over there and he felt it was his duty to go.
He was only nineteen when he was shot down over France,
and a French girl who saw the plane come down in flames
found his papers and wrote me about it. That's how
I found out."
                    And there were only thirteen

Silver Cross Mothers of Hamilton left, all in their eighties
and each month they put all their extra pennies in an envelope
to buy treats for the veterans still in hospitals,
the ones so horribly maimed they'll never come out.
"And," she said, "two years ago the French girl came over
to Canada to visit us. We have never been to Victor's grave.
My husband has been blind for twenty years. He was in an awful
accident at the steel company."

And an old Indian woman said her son was killed at Dieppe,
he was a paratrooper, aged twenty-one, and later
someone said there were no paratroopers at Dieppe,
she must have been confused. She said he belonged
to a Galt regiment, some Scottish name she couldn't remember,
but there was no Galt regiment at Dieppe.
A lot of people say they were at Dieppe who weren't
said an old retired captain with a red face
and the ones who were resent it,
but the poor kid went out
and got himself killed,
blown to pieces or burned alive
and even his mother doesn't remember when or why.

"The world's great age begins anew
The golden years return …"
And I ordered bacon and eggs and sent the
bacon back because it was scarcely cooked.

"With usura the line grows thick," said the artist
resisting his desire for quick returns, stretching
the lines of his mind to maximum tightness

and as the pipers faded in the distance an old man
carrying three empty pop bottles searched
through the alleys off King Street for a fourth

and a fifty-year-old security guard at Simpsons-Sears
was caught stealing $46.52 worth of underwear,
socks, sweaters and shampoo.

VII

Oh strange day!
Oh the strangeness of the day!
Oh the voices that stuff my head
like a Christmas turkey

and when they speak of the living dead
or the victims of famous atrocities
I think only of myself, I speak
of writing of course
and cowardice.

The voices of this planet enshroud me.
Your tear-filled eyes beg me to love
and every breath is my last

and again the lines move on without me,

the little dog bounds from my lap
and scampers across the floor,
the children laugh —

the dog is me, the children are me,
the floor, this cold December day
with bones breaking all around me

and my desire for darkness has brought me to this hell:
I become aroused in a flash
but that delicious consummate thrust

eludes me, I speak
of writing of course

and in the darkness I've sought and sought
I become a faithful oarsman
rowing my radiant hero back to Ithaka,

and these words are my only response
to the gentle goddesses who touch me as I sleep,
the angels who require no response
other than my continual faithfulness,
my lines moving on without me,
the oar's dip, dip, dip

with no reward, no muffled forewarnings of a distant climax
but the dumb image of a glorious hugeness.

VIII

I am wholly nailed to the holy
cross composed
of the four eyes,

> left eye
> right eye
> inner eye
> outer eye

That is why I call myself
Chreyest, one eye love.

But the nails pierce no flesh
and I bleed from the wrong holes.

"Why do some people have red lines
in their eyes?"

Consider the lilies of the field.
They have no eyes.

Keep your eyes crossed
at the Calvary Stampede.

IX

The task is to define the task in simple terms:
echo, echo, echo
> *All that I give I save*
> *All that I hoard I lose,*
said the female saint who wisely remained anonymous
so she wouldn't be continually pestered by the lame
which was a decidedly unsaintly reason
and whose book will last as long as readers, searching
for hints on the resolution of her early sexual problems,
are tolerant enough to have read this far,

and who has traced the line, coarse or fine,
between the poet and the mystic?

Oh, Christmas and the cards whistling through the mails
vibrate with awful wisdom.

Only the dead seek wisdom,
only the wise seek culture / to destroy it,
only the poets
have difficulty defining the task in simple terms.

But the mad,
mad ladies and mad gentlemen,
that infinite double helix,
only they have performed the task
and their definitions circulate like currency.

In general terms the task
is to write with simple accuracy
whatever concerns not me
but that which passes for me

for fate has glutted me with splendid gifts:
love so intense it verges on self-immolation,
hate so weak I weep for hate-filled hearts

but see how boring this becomes
as it shifts from that which passes for me to me?

Boring, like wisdom: vague words
that should be avoided, vague charges
impossible to prove.

Boring-like wisdom boring through the aromatic night
into the furnace of flesh
                    no human thought has touched,
the inner walls caked with soft opalescent fumes,
where unidentifiable voices pledge to wait
for all eternity
                until the dream becomes self-conscious
and the great burden of dullness falls like the softest rain.

X

What drives me is wanting to know *where* I am
or is this my ultimate home? The soft rug underfoot.
Not wanting to sleep my life away:
but never in this world is Odysseus dead!

This is no way to write a poem
but this is the way I want to write:
a reliance upon miracle, a surrender,
a sense of intelligent mental forms watching,
watching through my supple eye,
losing my grasp on the moment
and being grasped by it in return,
a tool pointing not toward greatness
but toward the mystery of human greatness.

"But that doesn't explain why Homer
is so much better than everybody else,"
said Pound as today we say about Pound.

And Turner became obsessed with images of death
and encouraged the rumour he was a retired
admiral, to explain why he spent his days
looking out to sea.

Note: On this day I was interviewed for seven minutes
by George Hamilton on community television.
In a foul mood, "I'm here to promote my play,"
I said when he asked about my poetry
then when he asked about my play
I could think of nothing to say.
I was there because the players were going broke
and while waiting for the interview to start

I said to the young woman: "You look vaguely
Chinese in that lovely smock." And she said,
"I am Chinese, you numbskull!!!"

                          But sing no more
this bitter tale that wears my heart away.
And George Hamilton said to me: "I'm a
quasi-intellectual myself,"
and began quoting Tennyson.

                          And walking home
I prayed no one had seen the show
and vowed never again to be on TV
for TV is to me as writing
was to Homer, a new technology
not to be trusted, as scribes followed Homer
from performance to performance
transcribing everything he said,
the absolute poet of his generation
whose job was not to make it new
but to edit all that had come before
out of the selfless love his lines exhale
or not to edit but to improvise radiantly
and innocently as Telemakhos sailed from Ithaka
to find his father and his father's fathers
not of his own volition but spurred and inspired
by gentle Athena …

XI

Tania, Tania, as I was eating grapefruit,
was suddenly watching me. "I just love
grapefruit," I said. "My grandmother," she said,
"has a huge grapefruit tree outside her house

in Jamaica," and I realized she'd been watching me
because my grapefruit made her homesick
and she went in the bedroom with my daughter
to do a school project on Mexico
while I made toast and tea, another day

and a high clean wind came up and my younger
daughter feared the trees were being uprooted.

"Mind is shapely," said Robert Creeley.
And the wind so strong I thought it'd throw
the stars from the sky,
                                    but shortly after the storm
the snow hung softly on the windward side of trees
and stray leaves of grass in the fresh snow
seemed like whiskers on a smooth white face.
And at the TV studio my facial blemishes
were caked with makeup, and the tortured lines
of my face blotted out like a distracted reader
blots out the lines of the most excellent verse.

For the time spent composing verse is added to your lifespan
and the time spent on TV subtracted.
And TV is a form of sexual experience,
the feeling of being in the bright centre
of vast whirlpools of darkness, of tiptoeing
into millions of bedrooms simultaneously.
Oh, the sensitive microphones, and in bed
the gloom of the day censors ecstasy
and usura lyeth
                            between the young bride and her bridegroom
and usura forceth the poet to appear on TV.

Ezra's intuition destroyed him, his intuition
those banker buggers were destroying civilization
destroyed him, as TV's attempt to implement stage illusion
evolved into a system of lies more dangerous than fascist
propaganda.
             "All the soul needs is at hand, waiting,"
said this crazed man who gave the twentieth century
its language, and perhaps at this moment some crazed eminence
destined to do the same for the twenty-first century
is about to be born.

The cameras and bright lights gave me a headache
that lasted for hours.
And in the window
      of a drugstore
where I bought chewing gum, headache tablets
      and a newspaper
there was a sign reading:
                NEW RECORD
                ON OCT. 14/75
                WE FILLED 524 PRESCRIPTIONS

1977

Night of Endless Radiance

I

Night stares in at nature's wretched vacuum
and engulfs you again in your own absence
while reading your name on every little cloud
and the world is drifting drifting drifting
across the face of the moon, a former lover,
remembered from another ruined century
when originality was the wave of the future
as magic was the wave of the past, and soon
originality will become nature's zipper,
those exposed will be subject to abnormal change,
each image with its own little force field,
invisible till it strikes the fields of the visible
like rays of light from stars viewed by the observant
on a train heading into the northern light
and the aboriginal forest shudders with thought
charged with power to enter and alter anew
the genetic code representing the thinker
whose thought you most admire — hence the notorious
Japanese reticence to shed tears in a boat.

The night moves on familiar horseback
through the hoofbeats of ordinary life
stopping only to comfort the afflicted
and justify the ways of wealth to the rich
as if the heart which knows such fullness
couldn't bear to bare itself, and will only hide
under clouds of words unable to cope
with the nature of their power and must protest
such fullness in a blinding flash of flesh
and must refuse a moment's intimacy
for fear of being overwhelmed for there
can be no ambition, no argument

in the face of a thinker thinking a thought.
We are often moved to think about emptiness,
not knowing what we're really thinking about.
And you can only hope God will dress up
and become visible like a bird or snake with long
eyelashes and tell you how wonderful you really are
but this is what you feel about The Night,
a mystical mansion afloat in a sea of blood,
a mind aspiring to Nighthood, a mind
that can, at will, vanish, and reappear
thousands of miles away a moment later,
so one can choose a mind at random and declare:
"This is what it must be to be The Night!"
For the light of illumination is not an earthly light,
is not a light that anyone can chart,
no sea of light, no gravity-bent sky of light,
no light that spills over mountains like pails of milk,
no light that grows like flowers on the sea,
no light that points at buried pots of gold,
no light that one can detect and track like aardvarks
or enemy ships in the radarless North Atlantic,
no ancient pots of light on ocean floors,
no lonely little light lost in a forest of light
and hoping to be discovered and made a star,
not even a spark that makes a turbine turn.
There is nothing abstract about this light, it's neither
electrical nor solar but can only be called
a radiant blackness or even a black radiance
(like the mountains in the interior ignored
by the smug inhabitants of the coast,
a sudden turning up of diamonds
in the darkened card game of the unmined mind).
This is night's eternal radiance
which, in a moment's penetration, heals
forever the cancers of the modern soul

and plunges it into its own millennial adoration.
And there is only one test for true minds:
if they were to jump in the sea en masse
would dolphins save them without a second thought
and with them on their Quasimodo shoulders
disappear in the moonless night
bound for Ancient Isles of Splendour?

II

The night, the night, its splendid milkiness,
where does it end and how can I get there?
It spills over its own borders
until there is no trace of those borders
and not even the milky night itself silently
drunk with its own silent illumination
can remember where those borders were.
The stars are the night's stigmata.
Only the stars themselves in ordinary space
and the occasionally mysterious conflagration
shimmering briefly on illusory horizons
remind the night it truly is the night.

The night does not know what day it is
nor has it any notion of its self-illumination.
The night rides the earth like a true knight
who has found a thousand holy grails.
The night is mad with its own desire
to continue being the night (and sometimes the day)
for the night is so profoundly radiant
there is nothing else worth watching out for
though there is always the danger of becoming,
or being mistaken for, the day, also nice.

The deaf shall inherit the night.
Miscellaneous crowds of apes swarm
in and out of the night like schools of dolphins
crossing imaginary equators, like disappointed saints
disowning their sainthood at the end of their lives,
and the night is a spider who has built a flawless web
in the fork of a branch about to be pruned, a night
where demons demonstrate their dire straights,
where pies are opened and many birds fly out,
and pies are squared whenever thoughts fly out.
Darkness is another kind of light.
The night is all depth and no surface.
The night is a giant medicinal herb.

III

The advantages and disadvantages of existence,
the development of the capacity to perceive
consciousness at first hand or even second,
whether to return groceries you've picked up
at the market by mistake and haven't paid for —
these aspects of the "argument with the self"
form the basis for the cellular hum that slips
in and out of consciousness like a mirage,
a metallic incrustation slipping in and out
of the Dewdney radar field and creating
a ghostly wind that has probably cancelled
by now your memory of having found this poem
under a carpet of moss and pine needles,
the pages stained, curling and discoloured,
the visual music speaking of a magnetic reality
where nothing exists that is not seen, where music
and obscure tactile sensations drift along
peripheral halls and through doors of déjà vu

and overwhelm you with their antique forms
and you open yourself to further dissolution
for you are a hunting animal and must find
each throbbing moment and destroy it
as in your sleep you sacrifice each dream
on the sacred altar of your tongue once more.

IV

The advantages and disadvantages of having
a flower garden: how many rosy petals would it take
to smother a tiresome accordion player
who has been babbling on too long about your beloved
as if she were part of the dull murmur
bleeding under the world's linguistic veneer,
each cell in ceaseless argument with its neighbour,
each cell imprisoned in its own cell? Warden, treat
your cells well and you won't get cancer.
And the night bandits, instead of being captivated
by the beauty of your naked mind,
will be unable to resist your cries of woe
and with their passkeys will infiltrate the cellblocks.
For your death is a breakdown of all that is dull
and even slightly predictable, another mysterious reality
where nothing exists that has not been set in rhyme.

You are burning with a passion seldom felt
and have forgiven the imperfections of this world,
your generosity causing electrowaves
will break on the hearts of unknown dreamers burdened
with the creation, preservation and destruction
of tiny intricate models of the current universe.

V

An absence of music, not made
by blowing into brass tubes or hollow reeds,
an unforced silence, a vacuum strayed
from myriad influences of surrounding music
storming from the radiance
that separates each clod of earth
from a quietude of the heart, producing a music
too slippery to cling to or to apprehend,
it's moving slowly along the Really Deep Valley
and awakens the elk and deer with amorous touches
and causes people to be wobbly with desire,
the night a radiant mosaic of soft glories,
and a wounded man somehow gets to his feet
randomly from a number of possibilities
(every dream he has dreamt is fresh in his head)
like a fire line packed away in a fireproof box
at the end of a wooden wharf on a small lake
surrounded by a forest north of Sioux Lookout,
a slice of pepper pie in the sensational sky,
a map of Canada in the shape of a heart,
the Great Lakes are dimples full of incorrect tears,
a country of the open heart where serenity
is composed line by line, almost perfectly perfect.
"This perfection has become overly elliptical,"
sang the Happy Twins as hand in hand they vanished
over Sunset Hill, and you'll never succeed in your search
for someone who will understand your naked mind
almost as well as you yourself understand it
on days when you almost understand it.
Everyone knows it's not easy for you
the way butter drips through the palm fronds,
gangs of midget bandits ignore you along the length

of night's passionate beach, Sappho returns
bearing streams of non-specific energies
and no one wants to hurt your pride by telling you
your dreams sound as if they were all invented.
You try to understand how so much depends upon
the whispering crowds of time travellers
masquerading as velvet puffs of consciousness
in the middle of Service Station Nightmare.
"Only midgets have the intelligence to understand
this terrible public behaviour," they taunted,
and one velvet puff stepped forward, and asked
that his name, a little-known one, not be mentioned,
yet as he spoke it was obvious he was anticipating
the simplicity of his own unfettered ego, and when he said
he wanted everyone to know he'd be available
whenever needed and would do whatever was required,
one could sense a certain frivolity was mixed
with his desire to do battle with those who ignore
the soul-filled cries of the purest souls of the age.

VI

"These are the things they said to one another
under the rim of earth where Death is lord."
These are spells designed to enlighten the author
and these are messages written while on the road
and left behind to help him find the road again
when night has fallen and friends are few
and there is no room at the metaphor, nothing
but what you see in your everyday life.
And these are dreams seen in times of darkness,
private dreams becoming public and at play
with one's private views of public dreams,
those dreams struggling to be free of convention

then abandoning the silly struggle as if they'd never
found the world in the absence of those dreams,
the public mind struggling to create a private dream
and struggling to create the conditions of freedom
that would allow private dreams to find their own
perfection, for there is a turning point when the struggle
ends forever, a night of endless radiance.

But the night will always be haunted by a notion
that the morning will bring a return to an age
when everything everyone dreamt was as elegant
as the elaborate warnings Odysseus gave the suitors,
the dreamer returned at last to find his heart's
desire being pulled apart by the modern age.
And what dreamer wouldn't at least be a little shocked
and reminded of a maddeningly purer existence
experienced in some ridiculous prenatal eternity
by the sight of a golden Thracian drinking vessel
bearing a daring pattern of Negroid heads,
goat-headed snakes, acorns and armoured knights
appearing in her or his early afternoon mail?

New generations fall into the sea again,
alienated from beauty and proportion,
discovering they've been born grossly deformed,
but whatever action the individual performs:
dreams of unpremeditated grace.
Yet these are but the arts of peace, peace,
observing one's dreams with modest respect
— Alexander heeding his ancestor Herakles
calling him to the walls of Tyre —
a respect often impossible to understand
though capable of imitating the purity
of the pre-dawn period when the songs
of the forest birds and the cries of the sea birds

touch the soul like the lips of silence
until even the Prince of Darkness is enlightened
and remains silent, unbreathing, overwhelmed
with grievous remorse, shocked at the cruel
stupidity of his life, his bones white hot
and radiant in their pockets of intelligent flesh,
his inner organs moaning with remorse.

VII

The old millpond reflected the flowering
horse chestnuts on a blue spring day
like an eye, a watery, slightly scum-covered
eye. And at night, after the fall of Troy,
when the eye blinked shut, the flowering
horse chestnuts could be seen playing chess.

At midnight the earth glowed with fabulous hues
and a pulse passed through the soft forest
as if the air had just become conscious
of the sadness of unknown gods and goddesses
at having to bar humanity from paradise.
It's for your own good, they cry, tenderly.
Try to see things from our perspective
or, if you can't, from the perspective
of the centre of the soul of the earth,
for the Incas of South America, it was said,
were massacred because they seemed so weird.
It's time for a tide of coffee, and through
the window the greenish leaves of spring
are copulating like rabbits in the wind.

She mentioned such massacres in her note.
She'd never developed the habit of closing her eyes

when she laughed, and as she laughed you'd have
the pleasure of seeing her staring at you
like a wildflower, for when the heart is opened
each beat is the charge of a velveteen bull
and what instinct will be left when the instinct
for beauty is finally extinct? The instinct of tyrants
imagining they have something worth hearing
when all they have to do is learn to play nice
and in their speech you'll find snakelike figures
at the great doorway of heaven bidding you enter!
And so you enter! And suddenly you are back on earth
at midnight, the countryside glowing with fabulous colour.
You've been over this terrain a thousand times
and suddenly the road signs mean nothing
and as you decide never to return from heaven
you find you've returned, your heart is as hard
to ignore as an everyday chestnut in blossom.

What would the world be like without the eye,
the watery and slightly scum-covered eye,
a blossom opening on the green of a stalk
after centuries of blindness? The eye does not
snap open, it opens with the emotion
of a brain that has not yet been born
but knows its existence depends upon
a billion years of devotion to the idea of
congregations of apes worshipping the moon
and stars all born in the dawn of the eye.

The eye pops open like a pair of lips
and an egg pops out. The pupil is an earnest
pupil and quickly learns the facts of light.
And if you look quickly you will see
new-hatched ospreys fluttering from the
noblest orb. And this is what the thin king

was thinking: the mind is a diamond
the size and shape of the holy grail.

VIII

Your heart is the source of night's radiance
and music enters your heart like blood,
the heart a perpetual emotion machine
pumping in great relentless troughs and crests.
The view of the stars is blocked by a giant pine.
The Florida manatee weighs a thousand pounds
and its giant heart is continually melting.
And the seagulls of English Bay can astonish you
with the lazy turnings of their awful cries,
the cries the heart would make if it were beaked.
For this is the country of the open heart
where to draw a breath is infinitely strange
and where at times you'll forget that you don't know
who you are and what the heck you're here for
like a long line of monosyllabic footprints
tracking across the beach and into the sea.
But the music will enter your heart like blood
and rainbows will explode inside your nose!
And the sea will tell you of your lost instincts
and you will enjoy standing on your heart
as the night stands on the knight's heart
and sudden flares will illuminate comfortable horizons
which suddenly take to the air and land on the other
side of the pyramid-shaped fast-food outlets.
For the most unforgettable dreams are evolving
from a universe contracting, an intelligence
with a sword in its heart, dying, a universe
in which everything is also a garden
the centre of which is a giant eye that never

closes and a heart that never heals.
And what is most delicious is the loneliness,
most painful the persistent knowledge
that you have not suffered enough,
that you have enjoyed the sweetest realizations
while entire cities have been bombed to bits,
schools of dolphins sobbing with uncontrollable
sorrow, and you with your pockets overflowing
with plastic lips, each with a diamond the size
of a tongue tip at the end of its tongue.

But the night goes on forever, its dark
reptilian attention burning diamond-shaped
patches in the garden of cardinal sin
while intelligent smoke pours into the sky,
and someday you'll return from your sojourn
among the golden isles of mythic romance
and with empty eyes you'll approach your birthplace
and will refuse to tell of what you've seen
and in retaliation your childhood friends
will become like gods again. But you'll be able
to draw a face on the wall and the face
will begin to talk and no one will bother
trying to understand, for you have returned
in the divine night of endless radiance
which surrounds you and is closing in
like new flesh around a bloody wound,
your mind slithers like smoke through the crack
between an object and its field of space
and a little mercury figure bright as the sun
holds the world aloft from its hollow centre
in brilliant flame, with pride, as if it were
a giant globe weighing but an ounce,
and like two virgins on an elephant's back
night and the broken-hearted universe

experiment with each other's nerve ends
and dream that their flesh is air, water, fire,
and dream of an ancient world aching to be born
along the length of the most passionate beach.

IX

The night is afloat in the mind of the dreamer,
an unusual sort of night, in its way as unusual
as the night of the living dead, and it contains
a billion years of evolutionary starlight
and the soft light bathing her features has oozed
out of the pores of her poor skin like mist
swirling in the early morning hills. Her arm
hangs like a falling star. And with each beat
of her heart the earth cools and a spaceship
shoots off into interstellar seas, and somewhere
within that single pulse you see yourself
being born and dying, nothing to be excited about,
and you might see a man dreaming of mermaids
and keeping a Florida manatee in his tub,
for radiance gleams on night's imaginary surface
as phosphorescent chemicals glow in the sea
and the night's imaginary surface lies along
the length of the passionate beach of banditry
where your loves and hates are incestuous screens
on which you project your life. Here, in night's
magical radiance where you can dream anything
and possess anything you want, women everywhere
were laughing themselves to death while men left
meaningless messages for future generations.

The night is afloat in the mind of the dreamer
and the one-eyed light of an approaching train
becomes an illuminating flower from heaven
and the world is a station where such light
shines through occasional chinks to illuminate
the halls of hell. The radiant flower was warm,
with a passion that plunged forth courageously
into further dimensions of *awe* (the sound
the heart makes as it opens a little further).
Every day you age two days these days
and every night you become one day younger
for time stops when the sun goes down and the
dreamer has too many patterns to smash
and the quiet path through the quiet woods
keeps branching and before the branches
reconverge her life will be all but over
and as soon as one path is chosen it too branches
until she becomes trapped in her own originality
lost in a grain of sand inexhaustible as a star.
For the mind works better without clothes on,
solemnly flashing in the middle of the night
like a beacon of wild flesh, a wild blossom
blinking music into deepest space.

The dreamer is afloat in the radiant night.
Even her phone is off the hook. And the occasional
chinks were tiny windows in the endless halls
of hell where fear and dull convention served
as the cruelest tools of torture eternity
could devise. And the dreamer, mindless,
drifted up to one of these random cracks
in the amorous armour of hell, a slot
awash with heaven's intelligent light,
and placed her blissful eye against the slit
as if a voyeur's keyhole or the entrance

to her mother's womb and the wombs beyond
(after the sensitive orb adjusted to the light
she sighed and saw a burning vision of
screaming children leaping into sewers,
or at least that is what I heard).

X

Sunset is a time of consolation, sunrise one
of experience, and between the velvet rays
of night dissolve the mind-carved blocks
that damn the noblest spiritual aspirations
and create a prison for the most lighthearted
dreams, a tomb for youth, bottomless quicksand
for all that is quick. The blocks dissolve
in tremendous foam and mist and the human race
is once again united amid sacrificial feasts
and that which animates one animates all until
the origin of consciousness is understood
and everyone sleeps in one another's heart
dreaming they're reliving past lives,
arms and legs entwined like musical theories
unable to differentiate identities.

They are so happy happiness loses its meaning
and evil is a waxed corpse in a glass case
with crowds of angels in such solemnity
to gaze briefly at such embalmed splendour
amid sudden visions of copulating snakes
and images of Miss Universe contests.
Night is a planet blocking its own light
and the furious joy of angels in heat
enters the world like perfumed thunderstorms.
Old men on deathbeds finally regret

having spent their lives at war with their senses.
Watermelons left lying in the moonlight
suddenly pop like popcorn on the beach.

The night has fourteen rigid principles.
The night is constantly brushing its teeth.
The night is afraid of the dark.
The night blinded Homer on a bet.

XI

The personality goes down like a raw egg,
like a kid with new skates who goes out and scores
two goals to win the Stan Bevington Cup.
There's a certain randomness about infinity
as if you could reach out into the Novalis night
and grab a hold of any kind of magic.
As when you were a child beginning to read
there were mysterious curtains and screens of myth
receding into the brilliance of the past.
As when you were middle-aged, face to face
with indescribable fate, you felt like a
flipped coin poised in the air:
heads your future, tails your past.
As when you were old, the night kissing you
with the blunt instruments of succulent flesh,
and you regretted the patterns of your lies,
which reflected a life of dull convention,
a life predicting widespread nuclear warfare
by next Christmas and the Florida manatee
eats a ton of vegetation every day.

This is the night of endless radiance when all
legends and myths will be placed on instant replay:

Columbus spots a manatee and thinks
he's discovered a mermaid, the *Queen of Nanaimo*
pulls out with three short blasts of its foghorn,
and all is well, it's a pleasant world, as if
you're about to remember where you buried a stash
of diamonds in a previous life and it's all there
waiting for your recovery. For the beautiful dreamer
who used to live across from the Montreal Forum
on hockey nights would watch the crowds going in
and hear the roar when a goal was scored
and that's how she got interested in levitation,
for everyone takes a radio to the Forum
and listens to the game while watching it
and the players become illuminated, naturally,
and play far beyond human knowledge
as much as the intensity of their individual
illumination will allow and there's always
the danger of levitation, players suddenly
floating high above the ice as if it's not
harps the angels play but hockey, with blood
spurting from hands and feet and trickling down
the face of each player and sprinkling the crowd
like holy sweat, the crowd becoming hushed.
Night closes in and falls into your heart
weary with the burden of being apart.
And the movement of the planets, comets and asteroids
raises and lowers the hair of your flesh
and each star has a billion stories to tell
and a juicy tongue with which to tell each one.

XII

You are examining a leaf on a tree,
a grain of lust, a raw oyster, sensation
as it slithers down a throat of slippery blossoms,
yet the throat tries to maintain with its voice
the same kind of intimacy that exists
between a couple through years of careless love
or the kind of identity existing
between a farmer and his fields and the kind
of interfusion existing in cloud and sky.
And the mind expands like a bloating corpse.
The mind reaches out until it touches another.
The mind's shape is dictated by the shape
of the minds around it. The mind is touched
on all sides by other minds. The mind
is an eye at the keyhole of all
the minds surrounding it. The mind is a
transparent brick, a membrane enclosing hogs
and pyramids and covered with secretions.

The mind has qualities seldom considered
and can provide comfort in times of stress.
Indeed it possesses the ability to emit
spontaneous waves of sympathy and to predict
general weather patterns. It has an ability
to disappear, a love of appearing and disappearing
here and there, an ability to attract razor blades,
iron filings and like minds and an ability
to feel at any given time what has never been felt.
Or just that feeling of knowing everything.
An ability to entertain the night as a trained
bear entertains the crowd. An ability
to train invisible ponies. An ability

to love itself with an absence of passion
more intense than passion itself. An ability
to love itself unknowingly. An ability
to know and remember nothing but
that which is necessary for survival.
An ability to destroy itself. An ability to destroy
its ability to destroy itself. An ability
to record, erase, play back and fast-forward.
An ability to see itself wherever it looks.

The mind has never been mined! At the moment
the mind's love for itself disappears
the mind disappears and mythological
creatures come tumbling down over the horizon.
Columbus mistakes a manatee for Miss Key West.
A. Y. Jackson sprinkles condiments on a pine forest
north of Flake Lake. A bouquet of blue irises
bursts into flame. But before the mind
finds itself unable to ignore
the proliferation of coincidences
all the more touching because of their triviality
and their persistence of course. The hog's ears
appeared in the tall grass. You could see
enormous pyramids looming across the lake.

XIII

Night thoughts are bandits unable to resist
the beauty of the naked mind for they find
the mind most beautiful when completely naked.
This diamond the size of the holy grail
reflecting everything all at once
becomes a voluptuous magnet attracting
oddly exotic thoughts from distant planets

and again these bandits have kidnapped the naked
mind in spite of the great risks involved
for a band of radiation surrounds such nakedness
and as the band of bandits approaches the band
they must devise ways of passing through
without being dissolved instantaneously
into radiant particles of quickly dispersing
static and each new bandit needs more cunning
and this is how philosophy is born.

The bandits were weary. They'd travelled from
another hemisphere and were wandering along
the beach, sighing, cursing, wishing they'd never
heard of enchantment. And the waves rolled in
at their feet, wave after wave of natural radiance.
And the bandits sighed again and listened
to the collision of trillions of particles of sand
and the sudden subsiding of the curious crests.
And teams of celestial apes with high-powered
jeeps and rifles roam the countryside:
the apes of wrath, each ape with a diamond
the size and shape of the holy grail
on the end of his neck. And how they love
to kill one another! They hang each other
on ropes and tie each other to stakes
and then set fires. The moans! The screams!
The stars start staring and become startled.
And the pencil casts a long shadow
as civilization disintegrates again
and saints love to cancel each other out.

But the mind is never naked, nor can it
ever be aware of its nakedness
for the concept of a naked mind
implies the stripping of the mind's ability
to know its own nakedness, a condition

of innocence so profound the first thing to go
is the very notion of innocence.
And the bandits no longer felt weary.
They looked at each other and saw nothing
but the waves splashing on the grainy sand,
phosphorescent waves in blackest night,
waves insisting on being seen by human eyes
as if their glorious music weren't enough
with its moaning tear-filled climaxes causing
a tremendous shudder to fill the equinox
every ten or fifteen seconds along the length
of the passionately jam-packed beach.
For it is not the mind that proclaims its own
nakedness and perfect innocence
but rather that which surrounds the mind,
the new romance that moves around it
as water moves around each school of fish,
the waves that splash on the sand-witched beach,
and witness the sudden absence of the bandits
for the face that stares out of the mirror
is at least as alive as your own. The innocence
of a bubble that has burst! The bandits sat down
and sadly listened to each other's hearts,
and as they listened they simply vanished,
ceased to exist and only the waves and the sand
seemed to be left. Like the story of Ramakrishna
who saw two boatmen angrily exchanging blows
far out on the Ganges and marks from the blows
immediately appeared on his body. Then
a truck went by and everyone on the street
screamed but Ramakrishna merely smiled
for this was still the nineteenth century
and motor vehicles hadn't been invented.
Even the driver's blood ran cold and the
bloody hand of a baby fell from the sky.

XIV

Spring came early this year and produced
outlandish dimensions of beautiful banditry
much of it overly excessive
and there were the unusually radiant nights
with the sunset's afterglow hanging in the sky
till the fourth false dawn told the truth
and everyone slept thinking all was well,
never dreaming an ugliness terrifying
was spreading over the world with dozens of dead
and dying dolphins lying along the length
of the compassionate beach. And a ferocious
longing for beauty was being attacked in the ring
like a bull while the crowds cried and the bull died
and the spirits of saints hovered in the skies
and a butterfly vomited on Keats' notebook
and fluttered away like a tiny Pegasus
bearing a wagon heaped with tiny dreams
and the hog's ears appeared in the tall grass
and a pyramid appeared in one of the ears.
But only two per cent of the population
saw anything, the remainder in their continual
lust for personal glory (as people say)
and a blind arrogance that will never melt
in the cool radiance of the heart.

And people you have never met
but who could have been your dearest friends
are disappearing in the moonless night
while the forest labours to understand
the sound of passing motor vehicles.

And people you have never met
appear crazily in your memories,
hungering for acceptance, ridiculing
your lost emotions, and the quickly fading
images of a splendid lack of horror —

And someone you have never met
smiles as he stands there reading your mail,
preparing a modest meal with his one free hand —

While at this moment, entering your body,
is a spirit the size of a baseball stadium
as if the sewers of Hiroshima were flooded out,
with cream cheese sandwiches on small rafts,
and an odd ladder leading down to a place
where long-lost friends have snowball fights
in summer meadows and resourceful gardens
where in pools of warm fresh constellations
of human eyes stare at the starry sky,
and the moon like Leonard Cohen sings,
while the stars, lesser medieval rhymesters
sparkling like rare pop bottles from the forties,
whisper magic formulae into the ears
of astronomers adjusting their helioscopes.

It's possible people you have never met
are living their lives in remote Tibetan villages
waiting for you to pass through and be transformed
by their overwhelming beauty, a beauty
only you can see, so your life becomes
bent like light passing through a black star,
a warp that will ache and ache forever
and you can watch movies every day
and scan crowd scenes in slow motion
and you will never find yourself

or anyone else you could possibly be
for you're trapped in the trap you set for others
like someone trying to swim Lake Ontario
with Lakes Erie and Huron strapped to his back,
poetry a process for stabbing the heart with lines
of icy darkness, poetry the art of darkness,
and tiny people swim for the furthest shore
in the red glow of a Canadian sunset,
each frantic swimmer and entire universe
hoping not to die and laughing playfully
as his or her lungs fill with real blood
along the length of passion's peach-strewn beach.

And on this spot three thousand years ago
stood a naked boy, a string of fish in each hand.

1984

A New Romance

"We are from Europe, home
of strong and warlike peoples."
— Camoens

I

Will the stand-up comedian
please sit down. Will the poet
please stop breathing. Will everyone
get off their invisible ponies, please,
and gather around, there are empty
seats at the front. And the words
are far too obedient
as if they could immortalize
that which has no life but the life
that is in everything. Each word
with its own little parachute.

This is the start of a new
romance on a cold afternoon,
heaven's open-door policy
rejected forever. The family of words
came drifting softly to the ground
and took their places seriously
as befits the dignity
of all that pure intelligence
and they kept their mouths closed
like shopkeepers intimidated by the mob
and their eyes open
like saintly souls on a pilgrimage
to a place where an oracle
would be expected to open
its mouth and close its eyes.

And the poet on his invisible
pony was surrounded by a
mysterious group of words wishing him well.
The group was more mysterious

than even he knew. At least that
was what one of the words told him
as he held it in his hand.
The word then melted like a chocolate bar
in the poet's hand,
the poet melted like a chocolate bar
in the earth's mouth,
and the words continued falling softly.

Reality dissolves imagination,
dream seeks its own level
in the grey dawn of awesome stillness
and the newness of a new romance
glowing with the skin's electrical fire
in the dissolution of the imagination.

Your mother opened her mouth
and a dozen moths flew out,
their wings pink in the morning's
newborn rosy glow. This is what
happens when one ear listens
to the other in the loving
embrace of another mother,
and the words surrounding the poet
reminded him they were once
part of his heart and had been
released in an ecstatic rush
in a moment outside rhyme.

Why must one always speak
of the unspeakable, the invisible
glory that pumps our hearts
and triggers our lungs
in its own sweet eternity?
Because if one does not

two will never,
and the hardness of the mind
makes the earth seem harder
than it really is,

and the stand-up comedian
(now sitting down) reminds himself
he was once part of nature
and was released in an ecstatic rush
in a moment without a punchline.

II

He made a bad landing, the chute
dragged him across the farmer's field,
he cut his throat on the barbed-wire fence
and before anyone could get to him
he died, a cow looking on with unfocussed eye,
unseen from the highway where the poets
of the twentieth century glide along
on a Happy Holiday bus tour to Gaspé.
All this is true, though intended
to be entertaining as a sudden wind off the sea
knocking the great aerialist off balance
and he fell to his death while several people
standing on the one true ground fainted.

Words do not grow on trees but words
rustling in the summer breeze can bring
you memories of a performance of *King Lear*
when the plucked eyeball rolled quietly
across the stage and two random members
of the large audience fainted.
A warm young woman from Jamaica

and a cold strange poet from a northern city.
The two came to in the first-aid room
and they looked at each other
with the special understanding shared
by those blessed with a low
terror threshold, those
who haven't built an immunity
to human inhumanity
and the spasms of horror fluttered away
and they began of course to blush
at the bloom of a new romance —
a poem to make you wonder
about bloom's inhumanity to bloom,
pure self-consciousness at work
striving to make the world
a better place to die,
striving to make a truly great poem,
a true work of art lacking nothing
but preconceived notions of what
constitutes a poem,
and part of its charm will truly lie
in its tremendous awkwardness
and its undisguisable joy during
the hour of its ecstatic birth
and its obvious hope that some day
it will be able to stand tall among the others
and be walked around and momentarily admired.
For pure self-consciousness
by the exercise of what it thinks is art
becomes evermore pure and more pure
and evermore self-conscious
until it must consume itself
or stop.

III

There may be a few poems like that
but it certainly doesn't apply
to the whole poetic race,
and you'll notice how Jerusalem
rhymes with Hiroshima
in the bloom of a new romance
and the poet who said his poems
were truly magnificent
and should be in every anthology,
translated into every language,
unfortunately never wrote another
and his desire became so intense
it rendered invisible the beautiful women
who sought to destroy his ambition
and fulfill his ancient longings.
Life is not like that
but poetry is, they whispered.
And he said one of the Great Themes
of twentieth-century literature
is silence, the word's transcendence,
so he made that the Theme of his Poem,
for every poem must have a theme
in the still (still, still) of the night
(music from the nineteen-fifties)
and that object that seemed to parachute
into your heart was The Stranger
come to make you uncomfortable
though you are free at any time
to crucify him (with your silence).

Ah, for every poem must have a scream
unless it begins or ends with a dream

like our little lives
and the poet was determined to make
a poem so great it would shake
the world and make a snake
crawl out of the grave of William Blake.
So he took the snake and ate it
after roasting it over hot prairie coals
in the evening with the western sky
changing colours, and that night began to write
his way into the hearts of anthologies
in every country of the known world
and a dog came up to him
and barked.

Bark, bark, it said. Bark!

IV

What do we think of as we drive
the pastel highways of our motor age,
endless currents of mysterious people
each in his or her little car,
some perhaps refusing to ask questions
for fear of what the answers may be
on the last clouds of eternity
where dreams are measured jealously
and music is fought over.
Somewhere in a car on a long trip
a nine-year-old in the back seat
wrote a poem about a kangaroo
that mooed like a cow
and the people in the next car
dreamt of being movie stars.
Meanwhile, a litter of twelve poodles,

each strapped to its own parachute,
dropped slowly into the sea
as if a quart of sour milk
could turn sweet overnight
and when the nine-year-old grew up
she forgot all about the poem she wrote
and though she sometimes idly wondered
how kangaroos make love
it never occurred to her to find out
just as when she was a child
it never occurred to her that she
out of all the billions who ever lived
was probably the first to imagine
a mooing kangaroo although God
has imagined mooing cows
which is just as spectacular really
and who would not at least be
a little jealous of such a being
whose idle imaginings end up
horny in a grassy pasture,
wild-eyed in a slaughterhouse,
pleasantly palatable on a plate,
wandering in a virgin forest
on the shore of an unnamed sea,
plummeting to earth with horns
entangled in torn parachutes
like dreams falling into the minds
of generations of sleepers
and somewhere a sleeper has risen
and resting his chin on his hands
is watching the rising sun
and above his head in a waking dream
there are four sailboats, each
with different coloured sails, each
about to sail, and the dreamer doesn't know

which boat will be the first to sail
and as the watery beams of light
from the rising sun seek out
each dark corner of these dark Americas
and touch the noses of sleepers
from frigid north to tropic equator
and down to frigid south, the sleeper sighs
and says (to himself) this
is truly a new romance
and the boat with the green sail
slips out into the waves of light
while the boat with the red sail
and the boat with the blue sail
and the boat with the yellow sail
sit bobbing in the calm.

V

Small words floated down
into the minds of selected sleepers
and the sleepers awake, not knowing
why, not knowing small words
falling into the silent flow of pictures
had broken the sleeping spell
and not knowing other sleepers
had been wakened at the same hour
in the same way, and no longer
could they be referred to as sleepers,
and now the journey begins,
the journey that never ends.

What words will have to float
into the mind before the journey
ceases to destroy itself? The question

destroys itself for in any given unit
of time every word in every language
will have fallen to the ground
that supports the mind's bubble
which will never be illuminated
by anything in these lines
and will never be supported
by anything but the ground
which has always supported it
and the words in their little parachutes
continue falling onto the page
which will someday support this poem
(and no one cares what you think
about the writing or anything)
(you are only reading this on the chance
it will intensify your self-hatred
and perhaps transform it into love)
(as if the only thing to do in life
is learn to love yourself)
and the hardness of the mind
is grasped warmly by soft flesh
in the warm night that will never end
in the warm sighs of everyone's friend
while children fall and scrape their knees
and nearby adults ignore their cries
and if somebody somewhere is sick at heart
the night's heart flows with healing fluids.
The words walk along the ground
like proud little centipedes,
the full moon casting little shadows.

VI

The mind doesn't want to stay still
in the hour before dawn, the sky
is still, the earth is still though chords
from a guitar drift around dark corners
and mind starts watching its motion
and small metaphors rise from the plain
like small settlements before the dawn
of civilization. In the morning mist
one must be careful not to step
on crocuses and daffodils
and one must listen for the hiss
of man-eating dragons
and the palmettos of the Bruce Peninsula
are glad to have made it this far north —
they stand so innocently and seem
worried about their appearance
as if they know that if they don't
look their best tourists won't stop
to photograph them, though they also know
if they're photographed they'll lose their souls
and their dreaming is full of an unimaginable
richness on our own dreaming's far horizon.
Of course they do not really know they are
the northern pioneers, the first thin wedge,
of course they do not know, they lack
even the simplest form of consciousness
and never mourn their lack
or even notice it.
Said another way, they are the simplest
form of consciousness and never mourn
their knowledge of their non-existence
for there are forms of consciousness independent
of the relationship between echo and ego

and to be truly human does not require
that we find nothing but ourselves in all we see.
There are so many unused rooms, in fact
we can descend to the unpartitioned basement
where we can linger unreflectively
in a small space as big as the world
and watch fish push their little snouts
above the surface of the water and disappear
and where at our mysterious approach
frogs plop into pools
                          and dogs
come up to us and bark.

Bark, bark, they say. Bark!

And more frogs plop into more pools.

VII

Oh for a mind as pure and neat
as a fresh box of Kleenex or a roll
of Scotch tape or a hot roll
buttered would be even better
and any humour in this poem
is purely unintentional
and as helpless as a new romance
that shines through the blackest cloud
that rolls around the world
eternally igniting the purest hearts.
It is she who must be obeyed
unless we wish to suffocate,
it is she who must be served
unless we're content to continue writing
egocentric, unilluminated verse,

it is she who must be venerated
unless we're content to die
without having turned away
from our fascination with fresh graves,
without ever having wandered
outside the realm of our pathetic lives,
knowing yourself only as a
mountaintop in British Columbia
or a stunted palmetto on the Bruce Peninsula.

Have you ever seen a fairy funeral?
Have you ever held a palm tree
in the palm of your hand?
Have you ever wandered through a grove
of palm trees forgetting to search
for echoes of yourself, the moon
dripping through the fronds like butter
and the night as firm as a farm in France?
And have you ever felt as pure and neat
as a fresh box of Kleenex or a roll
of Scotch tape or a stunted palmetto
at the very tip of the Bruce Peninsula
and have you ever been an echo
of something else, a hot roll
dripping through the fronds like butter?
If the answer to these questions is no
you have earned the right to come and go.
The voice of authority, so self-assured,
will it ever nauseate its possessor
and make him or her turn from it
with great waves of despair,
the human body hanging on
to this poem, a parachute,
falling wherever it finds itself
softly into perfect reality?

VIII

The speaker must be effortless
in his descriptions of the indescribable
and speak with the voice of no authority
and speak with his or her mouth full
in the grey dawn of awesome stillness,
riding along on our invisible ponies,
and there must always be more to say
than can possibly be said
or those wonderful scraps of paper
will stop falling through the air.
And in the morning you can put your hand
out the window and the first scrap
will bear a word that will be yours
until you need a new romance.

And when you do the words will lose
their random nature and will float
on pleasant spring breezes to your ear
and they will prepare you for the future
by warning of all possible pitfalls
and will tell you what will be
on the spot on which you stand
a hundred years from now.

And the trees will shudder
and ripples will form on the calmest pond
and you will feel her presence once again,
and the wind as it passes through the trees
will whisper your name in dozens
of different tongues
and you will look down on yourself
from great heights

                and your heart
a highly polished perfect mirror
will slip out of your body
and into hers
                and her beauty
causes the earth to sing
and the dead come alive
and dance in transparent joy
and anything that is happening anywhere
is happening to you.
The tiny individual notes from the song
of a robin a mile or three away
fall on you like sudden drops of rain.

IX

Beautiful poetry floated through
the minds of selected sleepers
like canned music on an all-night train
heading through the northern woods.

Night is a long silent train
heading west with a load of corpses,
a tidal wave of blackness aflush
in the fields of weariness and hate,
and it loves to whisper magic numbers
to prepare you for your fate —

And as the wind passes through your mind
day falls, night falls, moon rises,
sun sets, moon falls, day sets,
night rises, moon sets, sun falls,
day rises, night sets, sun rises,

life has its ups and downs
and stars stick out their bright
red tongues like little ketchup bottles.

Oh night of endless radiance!

X

Oh for a God as pure and neat
as an inverted ketchup bottle in the sky,
a hot buttered roll, a Kleenex box
that could contemplate its own
creation without bewilderment
like a poet reading his purest
and most innocent ode
confident that his total understanding
and smiling at the series of personal jokes
associated with each line
but that would never work —

For God is everything the individual
human being is not,
The Other shining inwards
on the small smiling blackness,
the individual human being
awash in radiant night,
weary of hate and selfishness —

A grey horse grazing in the rain,
steam rising from its shivering flanks,
rain falling on your overheated heart —
The trees are looking at you!
The horses know you're there!
The clouds conceal each dream

you've ever dreamt!
The sky is interested in your fate.
And the fate of your invisible pony.

XI

Night fell, the wind fell,
your holidays fell, and an awful fate
befell the fallen emperor.

In fall an old man's fancy
turns to hate,
and as the soldier fell
he murmured war is hell.

Bark is the outer sheath
of trees and dogs.

The Buddha died of mushroom poisoning.
Falling, his body came to rest
at the point where it began to fall
and a dog came up to it
and barked.

Bark, bark, it said. Bark!

XII

You stick your neck out
and you get your head cut off,
the fellow's head falling
in a moment outside rhyme
in a poem that goes on and on,

a poem so lovely you can't believe it
and you know it must end
but you hope it never will
and you will forever cherish your image
of the night as the superlative lover,
its heart spilling over into language,
one who has given you his bursting heart
in a life so short and thwarted.
And the rules for writing are precisely
the same as the rules for love:
Be natural, be affectionate,
and keep your heart just a fraction
below the point of absolute explosion.

Love makes everything transparent
and the heaviness of heaven
falls over our corporal cores
and we find ourselves existing
in a poem in which a line
is deleted once each hundred years
in the light holes of outer time.
And a voice says: "Okay,
do you like it now? Are you ready
to start falling? And what about
the *Washington Post?*" And you
are startled to a certain extent,
thoroughly amused,
but feel no need to answer
or even think about it.

Ah, the instinctual need for intimacy
and the innocence of fresh blossoms.
The heart swells and bursts
and the earth regains the calm
it lost with the birth of the ego.

For this is a new romance
and nature's latest inventions
fall gently from the sky
and wander off without reflection
to discover that which they have
never sought, for they
and we are indivisible.

XIII

It is unlucky even to whisper
about this perfection, to paraphrase
a famous poet, and if you hurry
you can catch him on the talk show
and hear what you already know
and disregard this dreary attempt
to fashion something deviously beautiful
from the twenty-six compartments of the heart.

Something to rival the innocence
of innocence, the invisibility
of invisible ponies, the softness
of falling blossoms.

And the words firmly hit the ground
with a force somewhat centrifugal
rather than gravitational, as if
spun out from an illuminated centre
burning with a breathless purity
that has no human qualities.

Oh what bliss, to be free
of human qualities!
                    And to watch
the cars go by on the street.

XIV

And the tiny dots in the purity
of the endless prairie blue
grew and became jetliners silently
landing on the bottom of the sky
as you bid farewell to your old romance
knowing your new romance will never leave
knowing that forever as you move
the new romance will move around you
as water moves around each little fish.

"A new romance," you whisper
and a series of bubbles as round as eggs
leave your mouth and fall softly to the ground
and land without breaking, the wind
stirring them occasionally, and they
are you and the wind is you
and your eyes are as inhuman as the stars
that stare in all directions silently
and nothing can disturb their ecstasy
or yours. And off in sad distances
the old romance still lives
sucking victims to their foul deaths.

But down here all is quiet,
the sky starts here and goes forever
and every time you open your mouth
an egg pops out and floats to the ground.

And the poet has taken his ordinary broom
and is sweeping the floor
where lie scattered dozens
of members of the family of words
killed when their parachutes failed

and as the poet sweeps he eagerly
awaits the arrival
of the lover, and laughs
at his own arousal —
the sun and the moon laugh too.

Spring 1978

Country of the Open Heart

I

When the phone rings in the middle of the night
the toes of peace-loving deities curl like pigs' tails,
long-term vegetarians long for raw slabs of bacon,
and a naked voice enters the head, a voice from the
mountains that encircles the lives of the poets,
and the voice is as soft as the core of the heart,
the mysterious molten centre of hardest art,
a voice so human the chips (with gravy) fall
into the polonaise sauce of daily life
and the heart is catapulted into silence
by the sudden eruption of its own inhumanity
and the murdered beauty of the loveliest life.
On a Friday night at the Cecil Hotel
in rainy Rainy River with seven poets
sitting at a table with millennial beer,
the talk shifted to colour and it turned out six
of the seven were partially colour-blind.
And on Rainy River's fortieth birthday he met
while shopping for cougar knives in Castlegar
four others also celebrating their fortieth birthdays
though he'd never met or heard of anyone
being born on the same day as he
and the heart's transparent bikini.

II

The dog stood on the bark, burning,
in the oceanic night of oil spills.
The dog picked up the pipe and puffed it,
the dog was discovered reading Pascal
and drowned in two inches of rainwater

while squirrels and cats refused to help
and his last thoughts were of you
tied to a television antenna, your limbs
so long and white and leathery in the rain
and amid the thunder came your voice:
"Don't forgive them; they know what they're doing."
From there the sea appeared as calm as a clam
as the murderous mob embarked for paradise
for their first return in three thousand years
but they found it had lost its rustic charm .
and this kind of sentiment is an affliction
as awesome as the kind of person who can fall
down a flight of stairs without spilling a drop
of her mind. "So this is paradise, is it?
Be a nice place when it's straightened out."

III

Hands up those with hairy armpits.
Your heart is being torn in twain
by the banks of the river of the transparent
self which has perfect freedom to say
anything but what it wants to say.
Whatever became of Catullus's yacht?
All energy comes from desire's reversal
said Venus to Adonis long ago
(of course Adonis really said it to Venus
but it doesn't scan) (another reversal) and
the human race has awakened and now
must reverse itself and fall asleep again —
the grapefruit tastes so wonderful
between mouthfuls of fresh lobster —
and the holy trees still long to resume
their impregnation of holy poets

for whom time itself travels in reverse,
waves crashing out from barbaric shores
like radio signals from frantic planets,
shrinking into the past with vast intelligence
and the knowledge that nothing need be known,
crushed spiders becoming whole again
and shrinking into terribly tiny eggs,
drowning in a sea of ordinary light.
Apes drowning in a sea of butter,
lions and tigers in a tidal wave of milk,
giraffes saved by their long sweetheart necks.

The gibbons are butchering each other
at the far end of the Hollywood Canteen;
their hairy dead bodies like dying whales
litter the pool with ghastly mixtures of blood
and soured buttermilk. Fate hath a way
of providing such incredible spectacles.
And during the hostilities lobster
will not be available unless an unusually
adventurous gibbontrepreneur dares the trip
through the holocaust to the peaceful shore.
No plans have been made to chronicle this war.

And the river that runs through the centre
of the jungle where peace-loving tribes
of hippos toss grapefruit at each other
and their fabulous music never ends
or just when you think it's about to end
a DC-10 crashes in downtown Toronto
and your doctor informs you a giant tapeworm
has formed a cave in the centre of your brain
with care, with attention to all the details,
with obvious permanence in mind,
and is sucking at the back of your eyeballs

as if they were nothing but mammary glands.
And the reader's attention stretches lazily
at the centre of a hollowed-out poem
dreaming of the carnage on the beach
or the hollowed-out centre of Toronto.

IV

The heart hath a handle in hell
and holds in its lap a bowl of constant cream
that changes its poisonous savour with the changing
tides of fashion, but the blood that flows
in all directions through time's hemispheres
has its own knowledge of ecstasy and terror
unrelated to such frivolous concerns:
thus in the sea, when tides are strongest
the surface will show its calmest face
and the agony of cruel crucifixion
can lie behind the saint's most blissful smile.
As this poem, when it appears to be pretending
to give an image of spiritual truth,
is merely moving through its own nature
like a snake awakening on a spring morning.

Everyone notices everything, but no one
who hath not a heart in hell's constant cream
can understand the breakdown of the world,
or the incessant cursing of the mind's unhappiness
in the surprise of the world's merriment.
An open heart is a joy entirely
and is enough to float a mighty thought
or a mighty fleet of little thoughts
for under its furry red jacket
the heart is a fierce little mole

that can burrow forever in any direction
and change its course with the lightest thought
— so light it can never look at itself
and its very existence can't be detected.
Welcome to the country of the open heart:
concerto for poet, flute and harp.

V

The rediscovery of paradise was billed
as the Canine Caper of the Century
and why not? The entire Pacific Ocean
is a Spanish onion and you've never
found it hard to say where one ocean
begins the day with a hearty breakfast
and the other seldom fasts at all.
While the hounds of heaven guard hell's gates
and yelp and yowl with almost human glory
the ocean begins to throb with devotion,
the naïve saloon-keeper asks Mae West
to sing for him, you want your every poem
to be pregnant with the ecstasy of the age
(for to sing is to enter the western
gates of paradise where heavenly hounds
do shake the darling buds of Mae)
and in the planetarium of heavenly glory
a one-eyed lady reads a poem about a total
eclipse of the sun and expresses regret
that she and her lover would probably be dead
before the next one and Artie Gold yelled out
"Heck, the way I'm going I'll be lucky
to see Halley's Comet," and later his friend Fred
while on a flight from Vancouver to Montreal
noticed a vertical line in the sky —

on one side of the line the sky was dark
and on the other side light — and just then
the pilot announced the scientific name
for the phenomenon and described it as
"the line that separates night from day."
So on his next night flight Fred stayed awake
all night long looking for that line
but it never appeared, and having forgotten
the scientific name for that most essential
of all lines, he wrote a note to the pilot:
"Do you know what you call the line
that separates the night from the day?"
and the pilot sent a note back saying
"I don't know what you're talking about."
— Just think of this poem as a contribution
to the notion of contribution, an executioner
in a black hood full of inexpressible delights
singing a lullaby to himself while awaiting victims,
a chronicle of Empty Lives and clever brutality
and the road to hell is paved with dead dogs
and maybe the occasional dead cat.

This is your Empty Lives report
for Monday, May 28 — but first
a word from the bottom of the open heart.
Hello, strangers. Do you sometimes feel
Empty Lives passing through your Open Heart?
Not nice is it? Well, we have the answer.
Take it to the Lord in prayer. This message
is from the Open Heart Poetry Co-op where you
can find the finest in new and used verse,
thoughtless people stomping on tender memories,
rabble-rousing racists raving about recent ravioli,
and incestuous denials of wrongdoing.
A ridge of Empty Lives is moving across

the Sechelt Peninsula bringing feelings
of depression and hopelessness to the area.
Record suicide rates have been reported
in Bay St. John and Two Lips County.
Even this poem is about to kill itself
to protest in advance its lack of readers
and its inability to continue forever
in a universe of its own destruction
for it's impossible to imagine a time or place
when or where anything that exists didn't.
This problem comes from Incredible Woe
and what is your loneliness but the planet's?
And if you think this is pathetic
you should have seen the first draft!
You are watching a heart grown wild and strange,
a heart of inexplicable rhythmic patterns,
a heart of sudden coquetry sublime
and that heart is your sole possession
and don't think for a moment your friends don't
admire the detachment with which you observe
your heart's grotesque configurations
for its attempts to protest its sufferings
and the cruelty of the age in which it lives
and its attempts to assert its lost glory
and its attempts to rebel against its fate
and achieve victory over that ever popular
stand-up comedy team of Death and Death
are, at best, hollowly half-hearted.

VI

The blood that was used to boil the skulls
flows in every inconceivable direction
in the country of the open heart
where cats and dogs discuss the weather
and there are as many ways of fearing
death as there are of dying.
You may plunge forward courageously
into the madness of your life
but the sky is always full of snakes
and you're paralyzed by theoretical
considerations of human freedom
for a snake is a line of perfect verse,
there are no adjectives in heaven,
you don't know whom to love and the open
heart is a spreading pool of boiling grease.

Fall far away from sin and grief
for your mind is the heart of the land of your birth
said the sea pounding in a transparent ear
with the rhythms of sleazy fiftyish surrealism
and the heart is something the damned can love
with a desperate passion that vanishes with the world,
the question of doubt never reaching a climax —

All over the world the sound of corks
popping and dust rising on country roads.
Is this folk music? Can a glass
of ordinary red wine be set to music?
There is nothing that cannot be planted
but thinking makes it grow, this wisdom,
the only wisdom worth living for,
the wisdom of the wind from the heart,

the wined wind that will never wind down,
the unwound heart, the wound-down heart,
and the heart that can never be wounded.

The autopsy revealed a bottle of wine
had somehow lodged in his heart.
Probable cause of death: poor vintage.
Forever drawing back from that final drink,
civilization itself is the perfect epicurean.
He refused to drink to excess so she
bonked him with a bottle of Vichy water
(would you be annoyed if someone picked up
a raisin from the floor and dropped it in your
steaming plate of beef haiku and spinach?).

When a billion people start writing
someone is bound to write something like this.
He told her to count her blessings and try
to live one day at a time and you
set fire to yourself in the village square.

VII

The heart is a powder dam on that network
of black blood flowing in all directions
while the angels, well-known for their wings,
invisible as music of the future,
as energy which lifts the heaviest woe,
as the sadness of beautiful animals
and trees and discarded artifacts undreaming
in dim corners of the studied world,
likewise fly in all directions, a poem as real
as a blackberry bush, knowing itself to be
a part of music it will never hear.

A blood-boiled human skull in the dump,
tourists indulging in silly arguments,
the skull's eyes empty as opal rings,
and the skull waddles away as cameras click,
flooding the future with unfocussed images,
and someone throws a beer bottle at the skull
as someone once stuck a stogey in the blowhole
of a trapped whale and the skull turned with sudden
fear and ran smack into a wall of rock
like a poet stuck in the middle of a poem
and before the tourists' dull cameras and fine eyes
the skull transforms into a mountain goat
and scampers straight up to the first ledge,
glances down, then climbs straight up to the second,
and the sun goes down and the moon comes up
and the tourists strip and start howling like gibbons
unburdened of humanity's low IQ
by an extremely rare convergence of stars,
skull and mountain goat, dangerous
as a dream impossible to remember
in the open country of deathless art
where love will sometimes travel in reverse
so that it starts sour and ends sweet
and becomes evermore intense till it suddenly
disappears like a butterfly unpinning itself
in the basement of the Royal Ontario Museum.

A tale told by the King of Burgundy
who owns all the whales in the Western Sea:
Three ugly nuns — perhaps the ugliest
in all Christendom — were walking along
the lonely road from Aix-en-Provence
when they were accosted by a creature,
half-bear, half-goat, half-shell, who began
pestering them with terrible jokes about nuns.

"Why do they call them nuns? None better!
Haw haw haw," he bellowed, obnoxiously,
slapping them on their backs with all his might
and breathing foul feces in their faces.
And then, as if that weren't bad enough,
"Three nuns are sitting in the tub," he said.
"One says where's the soap? Second says
I don't know. Third says sure does.
Haw haw haw haw." Oh he was hawful!
And the nuns suddenly stripped off their habits
and showed they were really men in disguise,
robbers seeking safe passage to Marseilles,
and they abused that foul half-bear half-goat
mercilessly and left him half-dead in the road.

VIII

A dog is barking in the Garden of Eden
where the swans and the blueberry honk and bloom,
vainglorious reality is covered with moth eggs
and time is an omelet ready to fold.
The animals on the other continents
have perfected intricate patterns of war
but the palm trees are amazed at their sudden
development of dreaded self-consciousness.
Imagine, if you will, a sad old palm tree
singing "Don't get around much anymore"
accompanied by all of Ireland on tin whistle.
This is a poem to sadden the gladdest heart
though it won't get you anywhere important.
This is literary careerism at its best,
a veritable addict's dream of literary fame:
enough sperm to float a lonely canoe
along the leaky River of Broken Hearts

where each glistening drop of sparkling dew
is a perfect little human being
waiting to be wakened into bliss
or simply wakened by, for instance,
beautiful poetry aimed at the mind's
perfect natural centre, the heart,
opening into the country of its birth,
a country overrun by angelic warlords
and swept daily by golden firestorms
proven by independent research agencies
using narrow-spectrum occurrence computers
to possess a malevolent form of intelligence
and a subtly childlike sense of humour.

The blackberry bush flowed in all directions.
Oh how fast this poem is running —
a poem for filthy minds, written by a lonely
bar of soap melting in a pool of tub water.
One cannot claim authorship for a vague
intuition that if one continues reading
or writing something wonderful will happen.
You will receive a wonderful surprise.
That small tingling sensation will slowly
grow and grow until your pounding heart
will turn into a blackberry bush
and your eyes will open and you will find
all as it was when your eyes were closed
for this is the country of the open eye
where Shelley's glaciers will stare like snakes
and the sky with a sigh will defame your name
as nature ropes its way around your neck
like the tail of an unrecallable nightmare beast
whose grey flesh rolls like tidal bores
over rank after rank of transparent soldiers
with light streaming through their bodies —

the Light Brigade, country of open art.
And if, while in a supermarket, you become
possessed of a desire to impress your companion,
pick up a head of lettuce in one hand and render it
a passionate kiss then say, in an offhand manner,
"Don't you just...Love Lettuce in the Hand!"
And if your companion doesn't laugh
burst into great sobs and loudly proclaim:
"When I heard that women were more emotional
than men I found myself crying out loud."

The blackberry bush of naked nuns
is flooded with images of a mind peeled
like a skull in boiling blood, and a heart pure
and thoughtless as a dog's tongue panting
in the heat of a passing passion
and you shake the dog off your embarrassed leg
and scold it, saying: "You bad dog —
you don't see me carrying on like that,"
and you are astonished as the dog starts talking
in a California accent even though
it's mostly Labrador retriever and says:
"But you're not a Zen master, you dope."

IX

When it comes to the end of its current tragedy
the human heart opens calmly as a clam
and squirts you in the eye. When you come
to the end of a perfect night you'll find
a Sleeping Princess with tiny naked breasts
and tiny breaths and you say what the heck
and you kiss her and she wakes up screaming
and the cops come and arrest you.

The nice cop says he knows you from somewhere
and you cry because he reminds you of your dad.
In fact you're crying a lot these days.
You look at a falling leaf and cry.
You see a man walking down the street
with a violoncello and you cry. You know
you'll die without becoming Rostropovich.
You remember catching leaves as a child.

Night falls and the heart shudders in sleep.
Someone has filled the teapot with gravy.
A cat named Buddy is crying at the back door.
He is not worried about the plight of the Indian.
Buddy the Buddha Cat of Indiana,
the loveliest place in the entire poem.

But at the death of Natalia Corvino
the hearts of many shuddered in the sweet
light of dawn. Oh the agony. Can she really
be gone? For the greatest fear is death.
Does the cut earth forgive the worm?
To share love the wholeness of the heart
must be split perfect as a birch log
and tossed in the fire of poetic cliché.
Thunk. That's all it took! And the more
you split a heart the greater it becomes
until all death is settled in the death of the self
which can never occur except in the self's
self-torture for at the moment of death
there is no moment — only the open heart
bursting with endless laughter, my daughter.
Natalia was alive and now she is not.
Natalie not? Never! Aye that's the knot.
Fear death? Fear this thought in the mind?
These dumb onions are for death's dominion

and for children catching falling leaves
in wild waves of unforgettable nothingness.

Hark! The kitten cryeth once again.
It is cold and wet and hungry and afraid.
The one you love is reading this poem
and giant globs of saltwater are purling down
his or her inevitably adjectival face.

X

October mind in the sky, October heart
in the earth, the happy harvest is in
as it always is, and these humilities
are porters of the sea and land
teasing you with hints about your fate
like the angel lady who lives in your spine
and continually feeds you with her heart
and tells you that she will never leave
and turns all time into a supermarket
and all space into your own hungry soul.
The earth is a giant pineapple crawling with
maggots. Smoke, like streams of music so strange
as to destroy forever all concepts of lyricism,
rises from all the little houses in the mountains
— unmistakable and therefore lost forever
unlike certain mountains in books of childhood,
the childhood you see wherever you look.
And she looked at you from across the room
and later the room looked at you from across her.
Did you have a happy childhood, George?
Oh, her eyes were as buttery as burnt almonds
and the room was continually shifting gears
like that most wonderful poem, "A Sports Car

on a Mountain Road." Something you didn't
want to write all right. And so you won't.

Music rises from these mountain huts
and the little houses in all the known world.
Her eyes split your heart in twain and burned
each half black as Plutonian mushrooms.
Her eyes destroyed all understanding
in a solitude of oranges and cherry blossoms
in the rainy summer of 1594.
Her eyes were inverted nipples flooding
her brain with endless optical milk. Her eyes
were dying soldiers in an ancient war.
Her eyes were the hearts of unknown assassins.

But the imagination has a humour of its own
which delights in destroying your noblest verse
and farts in your face as you lay dreaming
of eyes that remind you of the first pair of leaves
on the first branch of the first tree in Eden
and your heart pounding with wild surmise
and her eyes were perfect lovers fated
never to come together and never part.
Her eyes were planets of negative desire
in a world where astronomy and poetry
can never part and never come together.

XI

The human heart delivers itself in the plain
brown language of peace-loving deities
and gives itself to inexplicably
erotic monologues so monstrously dull
newspapers have to be invented

far from the broken eye of paradise
frightful in cold feet on bare night
under stars as steadfast as standing stones
and the seasons have their seasonings of which
the least intelligent are most knowledgeable.
But the illusion of the heart's loneliness
is as pitiable as the heart's realization
that it will never be lonely again is glorious,
as the heart unfolds its hurt across moonlit
landscapes and the first of a countless
number of falling stars fall softly on its flesh
and pearls pop out like beads of sweetest sweat.

XII

These words will embarrass you forever
by reminding you of your memory's soft spots:
the hungry cat is crying. Reading is dreaming,
writing is being awake and John Keats is sitting
on the face of a dead soldier, purple and green,
in the parking lot of the Banff Springs Hotel,
June afternoon, everyone gone but the guards,
the mountains giant pretzels in the sun,
and Keats points out a long silent freight train
skirting the base of a mountain in the distance.
And death's breath carves a line of verse
while the pearl of great price opens its nose
and squirts you in the face. Seventh Day
Adventists, please read no further. Others okay.
So there's Keats complaining like mad about Shelley
and the soldier in the last gasp of his agony
has glimpsed a great happiness at the end —
language with no grammar but that of the heart.

The heart is easily bored and loves to read
books about war in Asia. The heart holds
a hundred-gallon aquarium containing hundreds
of tiny heartfish nibbling on the green slime
of former obsessions, and has a healthy respect
for its assumption of emotional imperialism.
Friends, the heart is no self-effacing masochist
although nothing hurts like a herd of hurt hearts.
And when day is done and the stars drip ketchup
and Hollywood corpses sail across the sky
the heart becomes insane with incredible life:
country of terrible sunshine on shipwrecks,
country of naïve poets and peculiars
where the streets run with golden phoenix juice
and gondoliers argue about ductless glands,
language evolving from inner cavities
like planetary systems from the sun.
And the moon bobs in an ocean of dirty dishwater
so simple even a child could put it together
and what a child hath put together let no
god prevent the environment from living its life
for we're all in the same wooden horse.
Inevitably, the moon marks the channel
where talking cats confound romantic sailors
with limited intellectual resources by offering
inexpensive aphrodisiacs.
One minute a cat starts talking politics
the next you have a dog on your hands.

Oh look! A nest full of baby ospreys!
The old photographer in the long overcoat
is assigned to watch they don't fall off their horse.
We're heading to the very limits of the supermarket
and civilization is more obsessed with beauty
than a billion elegantly fabulous poets

but no more than that old photographer
about to be murdered by the Mafia in the east
end of Hamilton, Ontario, in 1950.
The long overcoat is gradually adopted
as each generation is born less furry
and with less fury. Asleep: the loss of fur
necessitates the sort of intelligence capable
of inventing a long overcoat (the old
let's-pretend-the-statue-is-alive
routine) (the open overcoat exposing
the music's genitalia). You need
another line here. That'll do.

The opening heart of the country clearly lit
in radiant night looks back along the line
of relentless music obsessed with its destroyed
silence, and the wormholes it burrows in time
overlapping the grid composed of the lines
separating all the days from all the nights
— such an obvious way of measuring music
and time. Yes, you must have time to like
the present if you want to hear my prophecies
said the Lively Enchantress so snowy white
and little dwarfs coming out of her ears.
Dwarfs don't grow on trees, she said.

And the poem is over but don't be sad.
There'll always be more to read, to write.
Someday someone will read this and say
"I like the writing but I don't think I'd
be able to stomach whoever wrote it"
and someone else will say "That's funny,
I don't like the writing but I could have
devoted my life to whoever wrote it"
and a third will complain about the jokes

and a fourth will say "I couldn't finish it,
though I have to admit that I checked out
the last few lines in which I'm mentioned."

1982

The Cow That Swam Lake Ontario

A curious story is mine to tell
and I must tell thee of it.
It is serious and much more curious
than that multitude of stories —
so frequent they have come to bore us —
of household pets, dogs and cats,
who have been taken from their homes
and placed in new homes far from their old
and somehow by what stars we know not
have hastened back to their ancient domiciles.
Such stories by their very frequency
have lost their ability to enthrall us, to remind us
of the unfathomable mysteries of existence.
And this story is even more curious
than those less frequent stories
such as the one concerning the dog of Flanders
belonging to a man who left it with his family
when he was temporarily assigned to a new post
in a distant land. The dog vanished
from his home and weeks later discovered
his master in a land in which it had never been before.

This story, my friends, concerns a cow,
a member of a lowly race
considered unable to partake of divine grace,
a race of ignorant, dim-witted beasts
who only amuse us by their ability
to fill our palates with intense pleasure
and our stomachs with bovine bliss.
We have marked, of course, how cows tend
to become somewhat rebellious
while being led to slaughter
but this does not necessarily indicate
an ability to foretell their bloody fate
by any wondrous sense of precognition

but merely indicates the cow hath an ear
with which to hear the loathsome cries of fear
of its sisters who have gone before.

And we know that on occasion
a cow will try to leap the barricades
and sometimes be successful.
These are perhaps worthier specimens
with the insane urge to survive
more strongly etched in their genetic code —
the nobles of cattledom you might say —
but almost invariably they are surrounded
by men with ropes and guns
and seldom make it far away
from their fateful road to Calvary.
For unlike dogs and cats, the cow
finds it difficult to blend with its locale,
finds it difficult to move unnoticed
in areas where it is not usually found.
A cow wandering on a city street
would immediately arouse suspicion
and you seldom see signs in stores
saying no cows allowed.
Of course these sentiments would be invalid
in some parts of the world such as India
where the cow is rightfully honoured
but in the part of the world in which I write
the very word *cow* is an epithet frequently hurled
at a slovenly, unkempt woman,
one who usually lacks even the cow's facility
for giving its lovely products to the world.

Anyway, on the evening of October 11 —
I remember it well for it was my birthday —
I was in a rented motorboat fishing for salmon

on Lake Ontario just beyond the Burlington Canal
through which giant Great Lakes steamers
in fact huge ships from all around the world
enter the factory-lined waters of Hamilton Harbour
when I heard what I thought was a salmon
skipping along on the surface as they often do
and turning I was surprised to see
a bovine head, with two shining horns
and two eyes as full and calm as fresh-plucked plums,
ploughing steadfastly through the starry waves
heading, and for this I checked map and compass,
in the direction of Prince Edward County
that semi-island on the northern shore
two hundred kilometres across the cold night waters
of lovely Lake Ontario.

I pulled my line and quietly followed
at a respectful distance, knowing the very presence
of an observer will alter that which is observed,
and I was surprised to find what must seem absurd —
the beast was proceeding in a line so straight
and at such a steady pace, without diverging
one degree in either direction from its course,
it made me think a seasoned sea captain
could take lessons from this lowly animal.

It was proceeding at maybe half a knot
as a full moon spilled a splash of light
and sparkled off its horns
and I lagged behind with my motor idling
at a speed suitable for trolling for salmon
until I was at a point where the bovine head
was about to disappear in the distance
and I kept at that distance
all through the night

following that awesomely purposeful beast
as it ploughed through the black and golden waves
straighter than the deadliest arrow
and as I putted along back a quarter of a mile
I sipped coffee and for a while
imagined I was the coach of Marilyn Bell.

And by the time the rosy fingers of the sun
took over from the slowly setting moon
the task of illuminating this strange scene
I began to feel a sense of senseless love
towards the cow I was so senselessly following
for I was not following it with the hope
of somehow capturing it and slaughtering it
and taking its carcass home for my freezer
but rather I was following it
out of the deepest curiosity
and a kind of non-anthropomorphic devotion
for I didn't even know that cows could swim
never mind swim the width of Lake Ontario.
The dawn was quiet as the night had been.

The sound of my softly turning motor
and the watery whisper of the swimming beast
had calmed my mind to a silence so profound
I could hear the slow soft thumping of my heart.
And slowly as we continued across the lake
in a line so straight I thought my heart would break
the dawn turned into brilliant day
and beyond the hypnotic head of this beast
a thin blue line rose above the horizon
and I checked my map and compass once again
and realized we were approaching
the shore of Prince Edward County.

We passed Wicked Point and the lighthouse of Point Petre
and entered a lovely bay known as Soup Harbour
which was named so the story goes
after a ship loaded with kegs of powdered soup
was wrecked in a storm a hundred years ago,
a ship so large and so filled with soup
the wives of settlers in the area
for weeks after carried pails of water
home from the bay and boiled the water down
and served delicious soup for supper.

The sun was almost at its zenith
and from my vantage point half a mile out
I watched as the cow's hooves struck shallow bottom
and it raised its weary body and stumbled ashore
and fell exhausted on the warm dry sand.
But it didn't rest long. It soon arose,
walked up across a narrow gravel bar,
its udder blue and puckered, barely swinging,
and slipped into a grove of maple trees.

It seemed strange there was no one on the shore
to greet us, no television cameras,
no hordes of well-wishers, no local politicians,
no corporate executives to shower my nameless friend
with free cars and other expensive gifts
for after all her feat was just as great
as those of Marilyn Bell and other mighty swimmers
who have conquered as they say the cold black waters
of lovely Lake Ontario.

But I didn't dwell on what might have been.
I pulled the boat up on the shore
and ran towards the groves of trees
anxious not to let the cow out of my sight

for after following her quietly through the night
I certainly deserved at the very least
to discover the destination of this beast,
to discover the reason behind her odyssey,
and if I lost her now I'd spend my life
torturing myself for having let her go.

Once I reached the trees I stopped and listened
and heard in the distance the crunching sound
of heavy hooves on the forest floor
and followed the sound until I came to a clearing
and there I saw a light so endearing
I'll remember it as long as I live
and maybe even longer.
Just beyond the clearing was a pasture
enclosed by a well-built barbed-wire fence
and in the pasture a good-sized herd of cows
and as you might have guessed some bulls as well
lazily grazed on green grass in the sun.

And there was the cow I'd followed through the night —
my cow as I'd come to think of her —
standing outside the fence looking in.
And as I watched a large black bull looked up,
saw her, and broke into a run.
And several cows and calves also came over
as if welcoming my cow home after a holiday.
And after sniffing each other's noses for a while
the bull, the cows and calves backed up a bit
and my cow crouched down as if about to sit
then with one mighty leap jumped over the fence.

The nearest town to there was Cherry Valley,
about four miles away. I tried to thumb
but no one would pick me up. I guess

after such a night I looked a mess.
So I walked to town and ate a meal
then phoned home and arranged
to have a car and trailer
driven around the lake
to pick up my rented motorboat.
And then I made a few long-distance calls
to various meat plants and slaughterhouses
in the area around Hamilton and Burlington
and after a few calls I talked to a guy
who said they'd had a nice shipment the day before
of cattle from a farm way up on the north shore
and from that shipment one cow had jumped
from the ramp leading to the abbatoir
and got away before they could recapture her
but they were planning to start looking for her again
in the woods around Cootes Paradise,
a little bay that flows into Hamilton Harbour.
You'll never find her there, I said,
and then hung up.

And so I went home and wrote this poem
without even bothering to wash my hands
or change my clothes. And now
I'm coming to the end of it
and as you can imagine I'm really tired,
although not as tired as that cow must have been
after its great escape from the camp of death.
And I know whoever reads this won't believe me,
they'll think it's just a lot of bull,
and not even very well written.

All I can say is this:
following that cow across that lake
was the most poetic experience of my life

and I just had to write a poem about it.
And maybe that great escape and marathon swim
gave the brave cow only a couple of days' more life.
Maybe she went back to the meat plant in the next shipment.
And maybe this time she wasn't able to escape.
Beef cattle are on the same level of anonymity
as earthworms, minnows and the untold thousands
who built the Pyramids of Egypt. The farmer
never would have noticed her return.
And her eventual fate I'll probably never learn.
But maybe, my friends, at some future date
I'll find her lying on my supper plate.

1983

Nevada Standstill

I

The carpet of snow on the roof below
is modified with sunlight and riddled with
wormholes from a rainfall so brief
and so sweet it didn't awaken me.
A chunk of ice loses its grip and explodes
on the roof of a car in the lot below.
"Am I nervous?" wrote Virginia Woolf
in her diary ninety years ago.
"Oddly little," she said. She'd just dispatched
a copy of *Night and Day* to each of five friends.
Of course I'm nervous. To be "I"
is to be nervous. Or even to be [n]ice,
overhanging, dripping, in the sun.
One experiences a pleasant change of scenery
and has no desire to return to the old.
"I'm very impressed but I'm also distracted
with all my ideas," V. said. "For unless
I can put some weight into this book,
it'll have no interest." The following day
she boosted Louie's wages to fifteen shillings
and decided to read all of Dante: Reading
is the only thing worth living for, except
for thinking, except for the nearly unbearable
joy and honour of bearing consciousness,
like a chalice filled to the brim with an unknown
vintage so mysterious and potent it smokes.
And it seems to emit ancient music, the music
of V., not writing today but thinking of it.

II

You're young and you think your mother's perfect.
That's omniscience. As if we were born
knowing about Virginia Woolf's diaries.
Women here and there and now and then
are giving birth to babies who will one day
care to know who wrote what at this moment.
People care to know the oddest things.
Some have been programmed to read those lines.
That would be the only explanation.
Plato had his cave, we have our soundproof
air-conditioned technician's booth
frantically pressing buttons all our lives.

One need not read a newspaper to know
the world used to be flat, now it's round,
and poetry need not rhyme, at least not now,
and eventually the world will be flat again.

III

Someone has written nasty things in the Bible:
"We believe in God, others go to hell."
The woman has a ring on each finger.
Two on some, and three more on order.
"One for each boy friend?" I suggest.
"No, I don't have any boy friends.
I had one but he broke off with me."
You feel dizzy, you've been driving too much.
You're a Canadian driving across North
Carolina on the way to Florida.

"Peace of mind is not all it's cracked up to be."
In your hotel you write this in the Bible.
Also: "No one will ever read this."
"Things like this are impossible to describe,"
said Hemingway as he steered the *Pilar*
through a school of leaping porpoises.

IV

Late afternoon, late January, North
Carolina: three or four small clouds,
pink and mauve in a salmon sky,
five slightly larger salmon clouds
in a turquoise sky at six p.m.
Salmon skies in the morning, salmon skies
in the evening, salmon for dinner, everything
riddled with wormholes and freshly dug graves.
I'd rather have a freshly painted picture.
A white man in a black Cadillac,
a black woman in a white Cadillac —
born-again investment counsellors with
fraudulent get-rich born-again schemes.
Everything is riddled with wormholes.

Ignorance of music, all is vanity.
Nine girls playing trumpets in a dream.
All the way to Key West we were trying
to decide if a blank line should go here....

V

Don't ever try to write about this.
Things like this are impossible to explain.
Let's do the Nevada Standstill, it's so nice.
A blank impossibility of poetry,
a blank line, a new stanza. The stingrays
at the aquarium yelping like puppies
as they leap, their heartfelt mouths displaced
urethral openings. Let me be your secret
lover and I will provide a fake fireplace.
You have everything my hearth desires.
"I've got a load of love and I won't let go."
"Let me be your lover for the rest of your wife."
It's not easy to acknowledge one's own ineptness
although it does feel silly sitting here
writing when one would better off be reading
in a universe more solemn than mausoleums.
Fake fireplaces connecting two worlds
out of which our lovers tell their secrets.

You can only write what only you can write
(when the coast is clear) (oil spills or not).
And I'm happy with my little radio
which I turn on at random intervals
(decaying molecules of plain old dreams),
and I'll open the mike and breathe a line or two
designed to remind myself of stale bread.
Every little squabble romantic or poetic
has the potential of becoming a nuclear fireball
and all our yesterdays are yellow brick roads
leading us from whomever we think we are.
One has been everywhere except in the spot
where no one else has ever been, it seems.

One never gets too old for low-tech forms
of information processing set spinning
in the darkest corners of our mindlessness
by an ancient dying god long past the point
of having will enough to destroy himself.

Taking yourself too seriously is permitted.
Wearing cowboy boots simply means
they were handy, a good buy, stolen.

VI

In Canada the slow are in the fast lane.
No wonder I'm so nervous. I do a full
day's work in less than thirty seconds.
Afternoons stretch out like rubber bands.
Everyone will be beautiful someday.
Anything we believe will come true.
The world is riddled with wormholes and so
we must work in a manner less perverse.
Let's refuse to add anything to the world's
supply of infidelity and infelicity.
We wish to die with a smile on our face.
Embarrassing how we used to fear oblivion.
Now we walk hand in hand towards our home.
No one minds dying with a smile on his face.
Next title: Please Be Prepared to Stop.

Now we walk hand in hand towards our birthplace
or towards the nearest cluster of galaxies.
Come on, baby. Let's do the Nevada Standstill!
The flower of the self, said Marcel Proust,
at fifteen, when asked for his favourite.
The smaller the oyster the better the taste.

The last graveyard in any swamp
has qualities we must not overlook.
You wish to be laid to rest in a civilized era
but it's difficult for diggers to make mistakes,
the sort of thing we find in Irish novels.
A poet needs a *nom de plume* these days
for all kinds of psychological reasons.
I've got it, said my friend, I'll call myself
Nevada Standstill. In the early hours
when we can't sleep anymore, we try
to dream up better names but we can't.
Not my style to say no to bumperstickers
or T-shirts telling people what to do.

You'd be more likely to see me in a tiny
dot in the sea wearing numerous T-shirts.
Saying "Drunks Against Mad Mothers" or
"Tread Safely on Mother Earth." Were there
literate togas among the Ancient Romans?
"Proud to Be Etruscan" or "Thank Jove I Live
in Ancient Times." Or "Proud to Be a Gladiator's
Daughter." "Christians Are People Too (sort of)."

Every time I fall asleep I dream of you.
With my last dollar I bought a dream of you.
Whenever you dream of me I fall asleep.
Why am I the only one here right now?
Savannah hotel room at three a.m.,
with my glasses broken and my pencil too.
Nelson Mandela not sleeping either, I bet.
This is the day he gets released at last.
Somewhere in Soweto a bright eight-year-old
is dreaming of becoming Prime Minister.
Doesn't seem to bother him that I'm dying.

VII

If I lived in the U.S. I'd have to live in
Key West, but I live in Canada
and therefore live in Toronto the Great.
Dave, why are you writing these things?
Why aren't you busy working on your
Amazing Oriental Truth Secrets?
Nelson Mandela is free, why not you?
You've never been to Nevada and you've never
stood still. You've never even played golf.
Nevada Bob's Discount Shorts and Shirts.
Terribly tired of billboards. T-shirts. Togas.
Telling people what to do about signs.
Saying "slow" or "stop." Just say no to
"at a certain fundamental level,"
"somewhere deep inside in my heart of hearts."
Just say no to the war on drugs.
And no to bumper stickers and broken hearts.

VIII

The dreams you don't dream are more interesting
than the ones you do. More interesting
is not to dream at all. Wake up and devote
your energies to fixing broken hearts,
saving species from sudden extinction,
developing technological gadgetry,
to leaving the world a better place
than your mother found it. Poetry's
noblest reward is humiliation.
Homeless old men in Miami Beach
carry large styrofoam signs bearing

indecipherable poems: "The government
squiggle squiggle children and squiggle.
Thanks for your attention, pussycat."
Failure focuses the heart, success deflects it.
"I want a car, I want a jet ski,
everybody has nice stuff but me"
(Dead Milkmen). Namibia needs modern
health facilities, but "like a drunk
in a midnight choir" (Leonard Cohen),
a poet is only interested in sounding good.
Politicians may wish to raise our horizons
but a poet only wants to boost his theories
(more interesting than sounding good
but one breeds the other day by day).
(For instance my house in those days was
a mess, and now it's a spotless mess.)
Philosophy breeds autobiography
breeds confession breeds consolation
breeds philosophy. Peace of mind
ain't all it's cranked up to be.
No more Jack the Rippers! (His big night
was September 30, 1888,
when he cut the throat of Elizabeth Stride
then disembowelled Catherine Eddowes.)
But we need scary stuff in order to live.
"There are no monsters are there, Daddy?"

Carcinomas the size of golf balls regularly
are removed from the legs of residents
(of Nevada). Having too much to say
can spoil a perfectly good poem.
Occult connections to poetry and cancer.
Without poetry there would be no
underground nuclear tests.
One too many nuclear explosions

and all the poetry is gone! The seagulls
are barking like over-pampered Pekinese
and the full moon illuminates the boats in the bay.

IX

You have now entered the timeless dimension
of your own being. You'll never guess (no matter
how many decades I wait) so I'll tell you:
I'm a fan of fifties jazz and forties.
Played every instrument in my mind.
Close personal friend of Max Roach.
No Yoko Onos, they hadn't been invented.
Just me and Max. Whatever happened I'm there,
a solitary man with one good eye.

It's hard to write when you're drowsing in a
shallow pool of goldfish. Even harder,
composing electronic music in such a state.
Some people watch television all the time.
Some people think they see music, sometimes.
Some people think they are Leonard Cohen.
Each of us is a Chartres Cathedral, let's not
kill each other unless we truly have to.
I'd give anything to write poetry.
I'd sacrifice myself to hungry butterflies
if I could write just one great poem!
The gods don't trust me, they think I'm lying.
It's okay to tell small lies in a poem.
One person's big lie is another's small.
One always lies (to A.) in order to be
truthful (to B.) (when A. and B. are the same).

Do you C. what I mean? Poets must kill
any desire they may have to have something
to show for all their other desires as well.
Llitsdnats Adaven. Oh to be in Nevada
now that the ninety-ninth century is here!
In Nevada you just go down to the corner store
for a six-pack of radioactive isotopes.
It's simple to apply to the government.
Just say no to the war on drugs,
yes to the war on sanity.
A lonely woman's dying. She won't allow
her children to come to see her, and her husband
is also dying and he won't let her come
to see him (he lets everyone else visit).
There are many brides of Frankenstein.
Nature just ain't natural. Don't let me tell you
what to do, but just in case you forget
life is wonderful, but nobody knows
much about the alternatives.

X

It's better in Nevada. Nevada's for livers.
Just flip a NEV and then flip an ADA.
A flip is worthy of flying over Nevada.
The dead drive us nuts with their complaints.
The dead made me do it. Cemeteries
will be the place to go to hear music.
The whole world went on a hunger strike.
Except for the friendly folks from Nevada.

Nevada means DON'T GO THERE, called that
long before it was such a nightmare.
You go there to gamble, and you gamble to go there.

I am Nevada and when I try to stand still
no matter how hard I try I notice I'm not.
I'm standing in a spotlight of my own,
swaying slightly. A radiance apparently
stemming from a hidden source above.
I'm driving towards Nevada, the car's owner
is "looking over my shoulder." The steering wheel
is my organ of perception. If I drive poorly
the owner will somehow know and I'll be forced
to drive lonely night roads forever till
I get it right, till I truly get it right.

1990

Cow Swims Lake Ontario

Or,

The Case of the Waterlogged Quadruped

for unhappy people everywhere

"It is too often forgotten that just as a bad man is nevertheless a
man, so a bad poet is nevertheless a poet."
— G. K. Chesterton, *The Napoleon of Notting Hill*

I had a perspicacious pup who woke me up
    When my house was burning down
I had a quick-witted cat who found her way back
    From the other side of town.

But cows are not thought to be terribly smart.
    It's hard to get them to heel.
They won't fetch sticks or do any tricks.
    You can't teach them to honk like a seal.

Cows are nice but they don't catch mice.
    They won't play hide-and-seek.
They'll knock over a pail with a flick of the tail
    But they can't spell *Mozambique.*

When young a cow is called a calf.
    Calves love to run and play.
But I never saw a calf laugh
    Or stare up at the Milky Way.

I once saw a cow in yellow boots,
    Another with a spiral horn.
But cows spend all day devouring hay
    Never wondering why they were born.

If a cow could talk I bet she'd say:
    "It's not easy being me.
I'm so overweight I can't find a mate
    And I can never really be free.

"I'm loved for my meat, I can't walk down the street
    Without being grabbed, roped or shot.
I'm not cute, I'm not pretty, I'm not even sweet
    And that's why I'm so distraught.

"If I followed a cat or a dog through a door
        In a shopping mall let's say
The dog or the cat would go free as a bee
        But I would be carted away.

"I'd be poked and prodded and put in the back
        Of a truck with other cows.
And then we'd be sent straight back to the farm.
        Or maybe to the slaughterhouse."

So this is the way a cow might talk
        But cows can't talk, that's true.
A dog can yelp and yip and yap
        But a cow can only moo.

A bird can chirp and cheep and peep,
        Chatter-jabber, bill and coo
And warble and twitter and trill and crow
        But a cow can only moo.

An owl can howl and a boar can roar
        And the various beasts of the zoo
Can perform all sorts of snickers and snorts
        But a cow can only moo.

They're not very thrilled about being killed
        As they stand there chewing their cud.
But they just keep standing there waiting their turn
        And ignoring the smell of the blood.

Yet now and then in the *Animal News*
        You'll hear of a cow of note
One with enough sense to leap the fence
        When they're about to slit her throat.

In my winter coat out there in my boat
    One cold night a week ago
I was sitting there fishing with nary a bite
    On Lake Ontario.

On the shore you could see a tall chimney
    Belching black smoke into the sky
There were junkyards and steel mills, dumps and oil spills.
    It was enough to make you cry.

The name of my sloop was *Amy McPoop*
    And I was trying to remember why
When out of the silence a ten-pound salmon
    Went soaring into the sky.

It sounded as if the king of all fish
    Was leapfrogging over my prow
Which was all very nice but when I rubbed my eyes twice
    I saw that that fish was a cow.

A few stanzas back in this slack almanac
    I said a cow could only moo.
But by golly, I was wrong. It turns out now
    That a cow can dog-paddle too.

A fish will often skip along the top of the sea
    But this was no fish I'm afraid.
It had two shining horns and no scales or fins.
    This was a cow on a wild escapade.

Its eyes were as full and as calm as a plum
    As it plowed through a star-kissed wave.
It may have been dumb and it had a thick tongue
    But this was a cow that was brave.

It was swimming at maybe half a knot
    As a horned moon spilled a pail
Of light which sparkled on its horns
    And I decided to get on its tail.

I pulled in my line and took off my bait
    And got out my compass and chart.
That cow was swimming in a line so straight
    It almost broke my heart.

Where was it going, thought I, and why?
    I consulted my maps like a Mountie.
That cow was swimming straighter than a freighter
    Towards Prince Edward County.

Have you ever dreamed of a cow like that
    Who would slip away from Death Row,
Who would be so intense she would leap a fence
    And run away like Pinocchio?

But no puppet was this, it was more like a fish
    A-swimmin' towards the horizon.
With me following along in my little old sloop
    All night till the sun started risin'.

I kept at my distance all through the night
    As the cow plowed through the brine.
When the sun rose I knew I'd fallen in love.
    I wanted to make that cow mine.

I'm no cowpoke, I didn't have a rope,
    And I had no plans to seize her,
To jump on her back, ride her back to my shack
    And put her in my freezer.

I'm not a fake, I enjoy a good steak
    With mushrooms, peas and rice
But I'd never dream of anything as extreme
    As putting that cow on the ice.

I won't tell a lie, I'll eat a shepherd's pie
    But I had no plans to subdue her,
To take her to my digs and jab her in the ribs
    And put her on my barbecuer.

Nor was I thinking of reporting her
    To the Slaughterhouse Constabulary.
Maybe I'm not the nicest guy in town
    But I loved that cow's vocabulary.

She could only utter "mooooo!" but I loved her
    And I even wanted to marry her.
I was so dim I didn't know cows could swim
    Never mind right across Lake Ontarry-er.

And there as the dawn turned into the day
    In front of my eyes so sore
Way off in the distance so thin and so blue
    Ran a line that for sure was the shore.

I could see Wicked Point and the old lighthouse
    That stands at the tip of Point Petre.
That cow had swum ninety miles, I suppose,
    But my boat had no odour meter.

When it was getting pretty close to noon
    And the sun was way up in the sky
The cow's hooves struck bottom, she shivered and shook,
    And she let out a bovine sigh.

She raised her body and stumbled ashore
    And fell down on the warm dry sand
But she didn't rest long, she soon got up
    And let out a moo so grand.

Cold and blue was her udder, so terribly puckered
    It barely swung as she walked
With a gait that was hobbly and a little bit wobbly
    And I just stood there and gawked.

It seemed strange to me there was no TV
    No well-wishers, no crowd,
No one to applaud my waterlogged friend
    Of whom I was so proud.

For let's face it her feat was just as great
    As that of Marilyn Bell
Or Vicki Keith or other swimmers
    Who at great distances excel.

Slowly she walked through a grove of trees
    About thirty feet from the shore
And I heard in the distance the crunching sound
    Of hooves on the forest floor.

I followed the sound till I came to a clearing
    And there I stood quite still
And what I saw was so endearing
    My heart danced a little quadrille.

There was a pasture with a barbed-wire fence
    And a good-size bovine herd
All standing there ringing their ding-a-ling bells
    And looking quite absurd.

They looked at my cow as if saying: "Oh wow!
        Where did you come from, gal?
You look like you swam across that lake
        From the very jaws of hell."

They all came trotting up to the fence
        And they licked each other's noses
They slobbered and snorted and mooed and cavorted
        And trampled on some wild primroses.

They all backed up to improve their view.
        There was an atmosphere of suspense.
My cow gave a moo and a little achoo
        Then leaped right over the fence.

Time to say farewell, but no way could you tell
        My cow from the rest of the guys.
They all stood en masse gobbling up grass
        And flicking their tails at the flies.

It was hard to leave, I knew I'd grieve
        (Although this is only a fable).
But she'd lazily graze for the rest of her days
        Providing milk instead of meat for the table.

2003

Danny Quebec

The trembling tenorman stands under
   the neons of busy Yonge Street at midnight
passing out handbills announcing
   the opening of a new jazz club;
the final feeble leap of a hooked trout
   sends rhythmic ripples up his wrinkled belly;
forest fires, igloos, and palm trees
   can be seen thru the glassy dimple
         of his stare:
his forefinger is unaware of his elbow.

Oh heaven what is your oath of unleavened
   purity to slide thru the tremulous
zoology of bitter flesh, what glimpse
        of silver solace may
I see in the meat above his feet?
   Do I pass and enter the tavern
to dream of further black swans
   or am I in veritable instance
part of his golden lyre?

   Oh send me my watch,
my chain, let the fields of
   wheat enchant me into
the song of the brook, birds,
   crickets, give me an issue
of your unseen parchment skin
   enclosure of sailfish,
   let me cross this street
passing thru cars and telephone
   poles, let me run back up
   and achieve at his feet the last
   gasping drama of slender
selfless bridgement of this
   upside-down concrete tower

to which all animate things are
   intricately attracted, to pass
thru my rock of remembrance,
     to be a hero in the
        Crimean War.

Oh what is this thing I am sobbing?
God, what is this the sickness called life?
Is this a cockeyed symptom, is this love?
God, Jesus, Love, accept my scrumpled self,
Let me snap my silver jug,
Let this harp dissolve,
Let me flow back to my tenorman
with unseen recognition,
show me my subtraction table.

This is not a syllable of slaughter.
This is not even a sonnet.
A sonnet is a symbol of sanity
for all my beautiful symbolizers.

Whitman & Shakespeare
were read by Ezra Pound:
Whitman sobbed on the lip of the continent,
Shakespeare sued the lords & laughed.
And Jesus considered Shakespeare a
     very enlightened man.
Milking his first cow, the city
   man is happy. —

My teacher when I was only 14
   made me parse *The Merchant of Venice*
while Gratiano screamed in my ear —
Everyman's daughter is the mother of God.

I left my shattered symbol
    brittle on the corner
and slithered on back to the parked car.
    With my head resting on the dashboard
           I felt
    my dead sister giving me her love.

    Oh hell and heaven, joy and subterfuge
let me raise my sword and
    cut off a chewable mouthful,
let my dreadful body drink
    from the shoe of Youth, let
the hair of my soul sink softly
    into the dolorous odour
of fishnet and pink.

    Grace to Jehovah and Heavenly Hosts,
I have thrusted my orchid thru your
       stomach and I shall
         do it again,
again, again, again, again, again,
    hair of my soul, soften & droop,
    you have been excited too long.
    Molasses & wine. Milk & water.
    The road is softest neither at
night nor during the day but only when
       it thinks it is.

Beauty, I don't know what that
    ocean is doing in your mirror
  but I have gone to the window
   twice and each time I have seen
that the snow is all melted
    and no longer smoke is
coming out of the city block
    chimneys since
       pudding is off for the day.

Inside the car, my sister kissed
    me on the lips and told
me that every design is one
   and that is pure and real
and holy and tangible
    and now six months later
in the pleasant shelter of
    my room I can place her hand
       inside my mouth
          and know that nothing
       is that once was not.

A concrete manifestation of individual desire
is the only object one man needs.
Nobody believes in God anymore.
A heavenly fire will soon rage thru
    this university
and the firefighters will turn to stone.
Nobody believes in one love anymore. —
Bodies will turn to pus and end
up on the legless beggar's corner.
The men of my city crawl thru
life, every self-action dedicated to
hiding their own inadequacies.
I am not complaining, I'm just digging.

Oh Joseph & Mary, show me your
   donkey, let me ride the golden
ass till silver melts; sun-stretch
   my liberty, gild my leprosy,
buy my limping sack of Eskimo hide.

Danny Quebec, it's midnight.
   Close the door on my city,
Climb the warming stairs,
      Dump your handbills on the
Counter, take your horn off
   Your shoulder, put your
Eyes in your ears and blow
      Loud stammers from your
Earthly vision, puke
            Into your horn,
         Drive me out into
      The morning vapours
And waterfalls, drive me
      Back to my shack by
The river, show me my
      Love in the sunlight.
I'll never remember you again.

1961

Bibliography

"The Poem Poem" first appeared in *The Poem Poem* (Weed/flower Press, 1967)

"The Ova Yogas" first appeared in *The Ova Yogas* (Weed/flower Press/Ganglia Press, 1972)

"The Poet's Progress" first appeared in *The Poet's Progress* (Coach House Press, 1977)

"I Don't Know" first appeared in *I Don't Know* (Véhicule Press, 1978)

"Night of Endless Radiance" first appeared in *The Art of Darkness* (McClelland & Stewart, 1984)

"A New Romance" first appeared in *A New Romance* (CrossCountry-Press, 1979)

"Country of the Open Heart" first appeared in *Country of the Open Heart* (Longspoon Press, 1982)

"The Cow That Swam Lake Ontario" first appeared in *A Pair of Baby Lambs* (The Front Press, 1983)

"Nevada Standstill" appears here for the first time

"Cow Swims Lake Ontario" first appeared in *Cow Swims Lake Ontario* (BookThug, 2003)

"Danny Quebec" first appeared in *PRISM international* 2.4 (1961)